STRATEGIC, ORGANIZATIONAL, AND MANAGERIAL IMPACTS OF BUSINESS TECHNOLOGIES

STRATEGIC, ORGANIZATIONAL, AND MANAGERIAL IMPACTS OF BUSINESS TECHNOLOGIES

David J. Good and Roberta J. Schultz

QUORUM BOOKS
Westport, Connecticut • London

Library of Congress Cataloging-in-Publication Data

Good, David J., 1950-
    Strategic, organizational, and managerial impacts of business
technologies / by David J. Good and Roberta J. Schultz.
        p.   cm.
    Includes bibliographical references and index.
    ISBN 1–56720–244–6 (alk. paper)
    1. Technological innovations—Management. 2. Information
technology—Management. I. Schultz, Roberta J., 1955–
II. Title
HD45.G579   2000
658.5'14—dc21   99–36598

British Library Cataloguing in Publication Data is available.

Library of Congress Catalog Card Number: 99–36598
ISBN: 1–56720–244–6

First published in 2000

Quorum Books, 88 Post Road West, Westport, CT 06881
An imprint of Greenwood Publishing Group, Inc.
www.quorumbooks.com

Printed in the United States of America

The paper used in this book complies with the
Permanent Paper Standard issued by the National
Information Standards Organization (Z39.48–1984).

10 9 8 7 6 5 4 3 2 1

We dedicate this book to Megan Good; Jonathan Good; Thelma and Eldon Schultz; Elizabeth and Roger Good; Marvin Hollis; Tim, Linda, Mike and Miranda Good; Carolyn and Tom Neales; Joyce and Tracy Taylor; Mike and Scott Richardson; Margaret, Dennis, and Brett Cooper; Loretta, Max, Kim, Angela, and Renee Bullock; Paulette, Joe, and T. J. Zazzara; and David, David II, and Geoffrey Schultz.

Contents

Illustrations

Introduction

Technology is a broad term that has evolved in meaning over the last few centuries. No matter how one defines technology, however, it is clear that its usage has historically provided its owners and users a distinct competitive advantage. Accordingly, one may own technology, from which an advantage can be gained, or one may simply use the technology to gain an advantage. Thus, in this vein, it is important to note that the invention of technology is not the only advantage that is provided.

As will be documented throughout this book, managers can profit substantially from understanding the effective use of technology. Although we are most familiar with those who invent technologies, such as Steve Wozniak, who participated in creating a user-friendly Apple Computer, and Steve Jobs, who is bringing Apple back from the dead (Schlender 1998), we are often less aware of specific examples of those who use these same technologies on a daily basis to gain or retain a competitive advantage. Yet everywhere we look we see these applications. For example, the wide proliferation of user-friendly software has become increasingly evident in creating strategic and operational advantages for users.

In this context we will demonstrate how the careful identification and management of technologies provide a significant advantage that for many managers and firms far outweighs the disadvantages imposed through the invention of these technologies. For example, in an absolute sense, did the Wright brothers or did C. E. Woolman, the founder of Delta

Airlines, gain more from the discovery of the airplane? In a contemporary business environment, therefore, the usage of technologies can be an efficient strategy, and one that calls for sophisticated planning.

The underlying purpose of this book is to examine closely the impacts of technology within contemporary businesses. As part of this exploration, we will assess the strategic, organizational, and managerial impacts of technology. To do so, this book will discuss such areas as the roots and directions of technology; how technology will change organizational teamwork; technology's influence on internal and external (for example, supplier and customer) relationships; opportunities provided technological entrepreneurs; and the influence of technology on marketing, employees, customer partnerships, information systems, and resource strategies. Additionally, we will examine the evolution of a new group of problems caused by technology and some of the general opportunities and risks created by its use.

To demonstrate the practical application and bring real life to our discussions, we have called upon our work experiences and extensive research within technology-based businesses and interviews with experts. In this light, through a variety of meaningful examples, we will demonstrate the advantages of the proper use of technologies and offer insights into the integration of technologies within business firms. Properly utilized, this book provides a strategic roadmap to using technology as a competitive advantage.

1

The Historical and Future Roles of Technology in Business

Contrary to historical perspectives of whether to adopt new technologies, the appropriate question of today's business environment is "What happens if you do not implement new technologies in the marketing organization?" Not investing in new technology may mean missing out on improved business processes. That can mean a lot more to the bottom line in the long run than other, traditional return-on-investment measures. As chief executive officers change their goals from focusing only on increased revenues and decreased costs to effectively controlling working capital and retaining customers, meeting those goals requires putting technology in a broader context (Murray 1998). The ability of technology to increase profitability and improvements, such as better channel inventory management, higher visibility of sell-through, increased customer intimacy, and better leveraged marketing dollars should be considered in the costs of not implementing new marketing technology.

A study conducted with more than 450 marketing executives (Tuck 1998) indicated that most managers are not waiting to find out the answer to that question. The majority of those surveyed already have technology projects completed, underway, or planned for the near future. According to the survey, more than 85 percent have automation at work, but in most cases only a fraction of the marketing groups is using the technology. Those who had successfully implemented technological systems denoted that they plan to replace or upgrade existing systems, indicating that this is a process rather than a one-time event. This chapter explores these processes and their effects on future decision making.

WHAT IS TECHNOLOGY?

As we noted in the Introduction, technology is a broad term with many meanings and applications (David, Pearce, and Randolph 1989). Accordingly, technologies offer a wide array of opportunities and accompanying conditions. To provide a common theme, however, as well as a single premise that seemingly applies to all types of managers and organizations, the focus of this book will be to define technology as human-made advancements that increase the effectiveness and efficiency of specific tasks.

Consistent with the evolution of contemporary business needs, we will chiefly limit our discussions in this book to technologies that are information based. Although a host of other technologies exist and will continue to prosper within business organizations, we delimit our examination to this focus because of three primary reasons that are discussed in more detail next.

INFORMATION TECHNOLOGIES ARE BECOMING INCREASINGLY CRITICAL

Cha-ching! That is the sound of selling more and selling faster with new technologies. Information technology (IT) has shown an inclination in recent years to be the basis of advancements that exist across business firms and is not restricted to any single firm, industry, manager, or functional area. Because information technologies can be economically and technically mastered by both large and small firms, the availability of IT is not restricted to a small group of users. Hence, IT is one of the truly available competitive offerings, and its application and usage is highly dependent upon the skill, knowledge, and willingness of the user. As a result, opportunities exist comparably for a variety of users of information technologies. Reductions in costs of computers, for example, have made the management of internal and external data more a matter of choice and less one of economics.

Second, IT has demonstrated consistently in the past 15 years the ability of a manager or firm to generate a significant competitive advantage. Thus, increasingly IT has become the dominant force in providing a competitive differential or advantage to many business users. For example, the use of video conferencing allows salespeople to meet simultaneously with important customers, while including their own product experts who are located in a distant office. Such advantages are growing at an escalating rate, as firms are increasingly seeking to integrate information technologies and strategic methods of doing business.

Third, although these technologies have increasingly been written about and discussed, and despite the contention that they increase the ability to compete, little is still known about their ability to actually increase productivity within the framework of the individual manager or firm (for example, Hise and Reid 1994; McDowell 1994; Myers, 1995; Van Gaasbeck 1993), as linkages associating performance and technology remain remarkably rare (Goodhue and Thompson 1995; Sinclair and Cohen 1992). Consequently, for today and in the future, the understanding of information technologies represents a critical tool from which significant organization and managerial impacts can be accumulated.

INFORMATION TECHNOLOGIES ARE . . .

Specifically IT has been described as the software and hardware that transforms, stores, or transmits information in a rapid fashion (Bloom, Milne, and Adler 1994). Although rapid advancements have been reported in many areas, few areas within business have been impacted as significantly as information technologies. Often referred to as IT (information technologies), this area includes a vast array of tools, including but not limited to personal computers, computerized databases, statistical packages, stored information and reports, computer links, video conferencing, and e-mail. "Computing to go" with notebooks, palmtops, and other innovations allows marketing employees to become mobile, working remotely with portable equipment. IT is packing up its act and taking it on the road.

Rooted in some environments, technological changes and advancement occur with little notice to casual bystanders. In fact, in some domains (for example, governmental), very large changes may evolve with little notice by community members. For example, many individuals not involved directly in military weaponry were surprised by the effectiveness of "smart bombs" used during Desert Storm. However, in direct contrast to such technological changes that occur with little notice, offerings of business technologies are becoming well recognized and prevalent at all levels. Consequently, many of these technologies are available in the open market, for those managers willing to make commitments to use selected technologies.

As a result of the open market approach to technologies that exists in market-driven economies, managers are faced with conditions under which they must either adapt to these alterations or suffer the potential consequences of utilizing outdated tools in an environment where competitors will gladly oversee their organizational funeral. Hence, because the knowledge and utilization of information technologies within business domains is generally available through an open market, constraints (for example, people) to adoption are frequently manageable by all types of firms, big and small. Consequently, managers who identify and apply appropriate technologies at an early point are able to foster a competitive advantage that can be overwhelming.

To understand the opportunities offered by such advancements, it is first necessary to examine the historical evolution of information technologies. From this basis, insight into the anticipation and application of a constantly evolving strategic tool is possible. To reach this goal, we will first discuss why technology has been historically important to business, from which readers are provided a first step into the strategic, organizational, and managerial application of IT.

WHY IS TECHNOLOGY HISTORICALLY IMPORTANT?

The significance of technology rests with the managerial abilities that have been enriched by its presence. Still, although the notion of managerial enrichment has always been true, only recently have businesses formally noted this point. Indeed, many modern organizations often see technology as a tool, but not as an instrument that can genuinely shift the weight of competitive advantage from one firm to another. Accordingly, we propose that managers incapable of seeing beyond single organizational uses of technology are those who will reap the fewest benefits from its use. Coupled in a business environment that is increasingly becoming complex (Webster, 1992), technology provides its owners significant positive advantages that include strategic, organizational, and managerial benefits.

THE EVOLUTION OF TECHNOLOGY

In examining the evolution of the modern era of technology, an observation concerning the cyclical nature of technological progressions offers interesting insight into the role of the marketplace in forging new technologies for business firms. Basalla (1989), for example, notes that changes of technology are primarily driven by the market forces of demand. Through the marketplace, demand is exerted on inventors to develop products. In turn, if profits are possible through the commercial application of these products, entrepreneurs will see these benefits, and, based on this, drive the product to commercial realization. Thus, the underlying development and commercialization of technology are governed by economic forces within a marketplace.

Consistent with the forces and roles that the marketplace places on accepting technology, the evolution of the product from invention to marketplace relies heavily upon business organizations. Specifically, through the history of technological development, a cycle of development and maturation continually develops, constantly being repeated (Morley 1996). In this cycle, the revolution for any given technology begins with the arrival of highly product-oriented firms, who all serve very specialized market segments. As this evolution unfolds, a stage of consolidation occurs, driven by financial and market pressures. In consolidation, significantly larger firms enter the market, offering more generic technological products to fill developing needs for these products.

These larger firms, however, begin to utilize sophisticated methods to market products that have become substantially more diverse. Driven by pressures, these products are soon converted into goods that are capable of being more mass market types of products, no longer designed to fill highly specialized needs. In turn, to gain more market advantages, these larger firms then begin again to offer more custom products, designed for specific market niches. Thus, in such an environment, technologies are constantly becoming market driven and are not driven by specific product requirements.

WHAT THE EVOLUTION OF TECHNOLOGY MEANS TO CONTEMPORARY MANAGERS

An examination of the technology cycle proposed by Morley (1996) suggests merit behind the evolution of technology that can be applied and evaluated in a modern context. Through an understanding of the evolution of technology, managers can anticipate what skills and knowledge their employees and respective organizations will have to have to be successful within their markets. Correspondingly, managers can use appropriate lead time to prepare to take and create a competitive advantage of technological advancements.

A close examination of technology-based products, such as computers, demonstrates a historical tendency to enter the market as highly specialized products, designed to satisfy only a small portion of the buying market. For example, the initial development and entrance of Apple Computers were based on the ability of Apple to become very specialized to small, unique market niches. Following Apple's emergence into the computer market, a host of other firms (Dell, Gateway, and so forth) began to mass market computers, often using more diverse channels of distribution to buyers (telemarketing, mail order, mass merchandising, and so forth). As these firms began to offer more mass selling strategies of computer systems, the buyers became significantly more diverse, with far less specialized needs. For instance, users were no longer confined to specialized markets (for example, engineers), as small businesses, families, and individuals were now included as part of the newly defined buying public.

As these markets became saturated, however, the need existed for the sellers of personal computers to again seek specialized markets as a way of capturing additional profit. Accordingly, manufacturers began to create new products, driving the emergence in this example of a family of new, smaller computers (pocket computers, notebooks, and so forth) that now have begun to appear. In another vision of this evolution, technologies, as with all products, move through various stages of the product life cycle. From introduction and growth, to maturity and decline, competitive pressures often exist to create and foster new products. Hence, in this vein, this emergence of new products signals a completion, and then a re-initiating of a new cycle as sellers move back into specialized products and markets.

Importantly, therefore, despite the emergence of new technologies, often on a daily basis, firms and managers best able to take advantage of these evolutions are those prepared to use the technology in such a fashion to gain or maintain a competitive advantage. In this vein, these firms are constantly seeking to remain market driven and avoid the dangers of being tied to specific products in any given market.

PRODUCT ORIENTED IN TECHNOLOGICALLY DOMINATED MARKETS

More often than one might think firms are tied to specific products. It can happen easily, and it can happen with little or no warning. For example, if a manufacturer finds particular success marketing products created by an expensive expert system, the tendency is to become overly reliant on such products that bring the most success. The tendency of firms tied to specific products, therefore, is that the entire organization becomes shaped around a single product or product line, and as with all products, the time is limited or finite in which the product can profitably survive. Often through the context of staying with a good thing, it is easy for the organizations to become overly confident in the long-term potential of a product that by its nature (technology based), is always short term. Thus, firms tied to specific products in a rapidly changing field, such as is characterized by technologically based products, should expect short-term and increasingly unprofitable ventures. This is illustrated where product life cycles of technology-based products are compared to products not having this foundation.

In the cases where firms are tied to products, managers are often trained to be responders to technology and not leaders through technology. That is, managers frequently wait for technologies to evolve, and then these evolutions are forcefully fed to employees, who resist changes away from the original technologies to which they prefer to remain tied. For example, in the early 1980s, many managers required that personal computers be physically placed on the desks of employees, with little thought to the organizational impact of these personal computers. Consequently, as many employees continued to use typewriters, despite the advanced capabilities offered by computer technologies, it was apparent that a great deal of resistance was met by employees being forced to accept a change they disliked.

Thus, when the environment changes and accompanying conditions change as well (customer demands, competitors, and so forth), firms tied to single product directions are unable to shift the strategic force and accompanying personnel away from this force.

MARKET ORIENTED IN TECHNOLOGICALLY DOMINATED MARKETS

In contrast to the product orientation discussed earlier, competitive markets are typically market oriented. That is, the demands of markets control the use and evolution of products. For example, under these conditions, buyers have the option of seeking products in which they perceive benefit and that satisfy their individual needs. If buyers begin to perceive a lack of benefits for buying a particular product, they simply refuse to repurchase the product. Hence, in these markets, the selling chain (marketers, manufacturers, and so forth) understands that alternative products can also be made available, if initial goods are not sufficiently satisfying buyers.

Following similar patterns of other inventions and advancements, information technologies were originally not market oriented. Instead, this status is the reflection of the development and maturity of the market, as well as those competitors who reside within the environment. In this market, sellers basically determined in advance what products would be right for which buyers. For example, hobby computers were constructed almost exclusively for a very select market. In turn, marketers made little effort to push these products outside of the initial marketplace (the hobbyist) that was determined right for these products. This resulted in three specific implications that continue to haunt businesses today.

First, sellers of technologies were extremely limited in opportunities to sell products to new users. As with other technologies, the initial cost of the product (research, introduction, education, and so forth) could be so expensive that such a strategy limited opportunities for growth because sellers were extremely wary of integrating new products into markets that may not be profitable in the long run.

Second, this approach allowed a small number of sellers to capture these technologies, and convert them into their own business applications. Although this allowed some firms to take significant advantage of this condition, others began a cycle in which they learned to construct a culture designed to respond to technological advancements and not anticipate progress.

Third, as technology users became more pervasive in the 1980s use moved away from only those who were technically skilled to a wider range of users. For example, many sales offices in the early 1980s had only limited access to computers and the accompanying information and statistical packages personal computers offered. As the markets became more nearly saturated, however, with information technologies, the people who actually used computers broadened enormously. Today, users range across all disciplines and job responsibilities, as the forces of the market have moved the management of technology away from inventors and "techno-nuts" (our affectionate term for individuals who are more concerned about the mechanics of the technology than its application) to those who use the technology to gain or maintain a competitive advantage.

Unlike these techno-nuts, techno-users are primarily concerned with the application of technologies. Although it is clear that techno-nuts are critical components in incorporating technologies (for example, bridging current organizational capabilities with new advancements) within the organization, they are very limited in creating enthusiasm or interest in encouraging the firm to adapt to new advancements. Critical individuals when the need is to integrate technologies throughout an organization, techno-users are specifically concerned about how technologies directly affect organizational responsibilities. Although these individuals occasionally demonstrate the in depth knowledge of techno-nuts, their charter is to use technologies. Thus, although always striving to expand the application of technologies, these individuals constantly ask how it can be used. Hence, techno-users are key employees who play a critical role in incorporating new business technologies. Without these techno-users, obtaining technologies and actually installing them organizationally is a significantly different and more challenging task.

WHAT MANAGERS WANT FROM TECHNOLOGY

In a market-oriented setting, the demands are not per se to have the best technology, but instead to get the best results (for example, profits). As a result, the focus is on developing and maintaining those activities that generate the best organizational outcomes. In this setting, managers should initially highlight the degree to which the utilization of technology provides the best opportunity to reach organizational goals. If it is determined that technology does provide this bridge, then it must be established how this advantage can be strategically cultivated.

In an exploration of all technologies and their marriage to businesses, we contend that the ability to utilize technology is important, but the use alone does not automatically bring success. Accordingly, the strategic inclusion of technology should be viewed in the context of what specific advantages IT provides the user (for example, managers and businesses). Similarly, if these advantages should diminish, managers should forcefully explore other opportunities generated through both technologies and other mechanisms. Under this premise, therefore, technology should be viewed as a strong glue holding the organizational mission to its direction. Over time, however, the glue must be periodically examined to ensure that its cohesive properties continue to provide bonding capabilities. As improved adherents enter the market, it is advantageous to use them when appropriate.

The basic motivator, therefore, is developing and maintaining a competitive advantage (Bharadwaj, Varadarajan, and Fahy 1993; Day and Nedungadi 1984), as the historical driving force (Clark 1954; Alderson 1957, 1965) that inspires managers to incorporate business technologies. It is the market, therefore, that necessitates that managers utilize technology. Unlike an invention personality, where the drive is to be the first to discover, being first to apply is inherently more critical within business markets. Importantly, under such a perspective of managing and utilizing technology, the foundation thought is that the organizational and the employees need to adopt a technological orientation.

TECHNOLOGICAL ORIENTATION

Critical to integrating technology within a firm is the degree to which the organization possesses a technological orientation. Specifically, we define a technological orientation as "an individual and employing firm which demonstrates the willingness and the ability to accept new technologies." Not limited to just a few employees, this perspective suggests that an underlying theme in the firm and individual reflects a critical tendency to want to try new technologies. That is to say, the individual and firm embracing this outlook are willing to try new methods to accomplish existing or new tasks.

To have this outlook, several distinctive qualities typically must have filtered throughout the organization. First, top management has communicated not only a willingness to engage in new technologies but also made the message clear throughout the firm that the adoption of these advancements is a basic expectation or requirement of employees. Hence, upper management must openly demand subordinates use technologies that the organization embraces. For example, if video conferencing has been purchased, it is assumed under this perspective, that the possession of the equipment is not enough to ensure its use. As a result, through training and assistance in scheduling and using the equipment, the message of technological usage is communicated. Further, by linking performance and rewards to the use of technologies, the message can clearly indicate that selected technologies will be incorporated into corporate activities.

Second, to adapt the organization to a technological orientation, a commitment must also exist to train employees as necessary. The nature of technology (that is, rapid advancements) suggests that at any time a reasonable number of employees will have insufficient knowledge to implement and integrate these developments. Thus, a formal commitment (that is, resources) must be made to ensure employees have the appropriate skills and knowledge of emerging technologies. Although in some cases this training may simply require on-the-job training, in other instances, more formal programs (classroom sessions, and so forth) may be required to instill such information. Thus, commitments to develop technological skills begin at the top, and will only be fulfilled if driven from the top throughout the entire organization.

Third, to remain a technological industry leader requires a financial dedication to be willing to commit resources early in the life cycles of new developments. Because early adoptions limit supply sources of technologies, the costs of these products are typically quite high. As a result, firms committing to a technological orientation should expect to devote relatively high resource expenditures to purchasing and maintaining contemporary technologies. In turn, however, because early adopters can expect to reap the most benefits of product applications, early adoption should be expected to provide a higher than industry normal return on investment.

Fourth, a critical component of developing a technological orientation rests on the ability of the firm to attract and retain the right personnel. That is, because adoption rates of any product rest with users being first willing to be innovators, business organizations desiring to become technologically oriented must find employees who desire to be innovative in their job pursuits. Individuals who are slow to change in life or their job are probably not the right people to place in roles where the tools (technology) rapidly change. As a downside to adopting this orientation, however, competing firms will recognize the advantages that this status creates. Hence, technology leaders should expect that they will occasionally lose key employees (techno-users and techno-nuts) who are able to transcend competitors rapidly through technological adoption stages.

In summary, the integration and acceptance of technology throughout the organization to enhance and enrich individual and organizational output relies on the outlook of the firm, and accordingly, the employees. When a technological orientation exists, the adoption of key technologies becomes much easier.

APPENDIX
INFORMATION TECHNOLOGY DEVELOPMENTS: IMPLICATIONS FOR BUSINESS STRATEGY

Robert W. Stone, Associate Professor,
College of Business and Economics, University of Idaho

There are numerous forces impacting the business environment. One force of unrelenting change is IT. The perception of information and its use have evolved over the years to the point that information is often seen as a commodity or utility. Any desired data, or its context sensitive partner, information, is on demand by business professionals and available to them at any time and place. Convenience, productivity, competition, and habit drive these expectations.

The development of these expectations has taken place over time. Major forces fueling these changes are the Internet and its enabling technologies. The Internet has changed many aspects of business and professional lives around the world. Surveys have shown that among young adults (that is, from the early teens through mid-thirties), access to the Internet has changed leisure habits. "Surfing the Web" has become a rival of watching television for leisure activities. The shift has been sufficiently large to produce an according change in the composite of advertising dollars spent. This trend does not appear to be lessening. In fact, in the future it appears that it will become a more dominant force.

The World Wide Web (WWW) in itself could not have made these changes without advances in its enabling technologies. The increased use of packet switching as opposed to direction connections for telecommunications was one such change. Another was the development of open systems employing industry standards replacing the use of proprietary networks. The Telecommunication Act of 1996 also had significant impacts facilitating these changes. Deregulation has accelerated the speed of new technology development in communications.

The implications of these changes for business strategy are several. First, the changing lifestyle and habits of consumers and employees will force businesses to adjust their IT strategies. Consumers will force business to at least consider electronic commerce as well as shift advertising efforts to include exposure on the WWW. As consumers become more comfortable shopping and interacting with businesses over the Internet, more customer service activities will be done over the WWW. As employees push for greater access to data and computing power in an anyplace, anytime format, organizations will face demands for greater communication capacity and the latest technologies.

The responses by business to these forces or demands cannot be, nor should they be, immediate and all encompassing. These forces and changes dictate significant changes in the IT plans of businesses. Yet, the adjustments need to be gradual with a maximum degree of flexibility because of the costs of making such adjustments. Costs tend to increase as the speed of adjustment increases. Further, because of the volatile nature of these technologies, their development and use require a gentle migration in the IT plan. Further, these changes are occurring at an extremely rapid pace with development in this area in its infancy. As a result, innovation is very transitory as today's innovation is replicated and extended into tomorrow's newest development. Thus, what is new today is old news in 3–4 months and flexibility is paramount to allow firms to adjust when new, unexpected innovations in technology appear.

The WWW presents businesses with a host of exciting, nontraditional methods of communicating and conducting business. In such an environment, there is no single, proven business model. Firms are experimenting with a variety of approaches or business models on the WWW. Some of these include on-line malls, advertising and client education efforts, and virtual stores via corporate WWW sites. These types of electronic commerce provide a dynamic arena, with many businesses not reporting profits from their sites. However, this is predicted to change significantly after the year 2000. Until such time, organizations appear to be using their WWW sites to establish corporate identities and brand names, and to acclimate consumers so as to encourage future use. Other benefits sought at this time include the testing of products and the gathering of research both on markets and competitors.

There are several barriers that need to be overcome on the WWW. The most critical of these barriers are the consumers' perceptions of the Internet's security and reliability. Many consumers doubt the security of on-line business transactions. In some cases, this is warranted because some WWW sites do not use secure technologies. In addition, some Internet browsers lack built-in security. Further, at times Internet connections and sites are not reliable, meaning that at times consumers cannot access the WWW or individual WWW sites. These issues require time and positive consumer experiences to solve.

Regardless of these barriers and the unresolved business case for WWW use by business organizations, the WWW is a force that must be addressed. Firms must invest in the technologies and WWW approaches that best suit their products and strategies. The investment needs to be justified initially not on hard returns, but rather the soft benefits of expected future gains as the firm researches and identifies its place on the WWW.

2

Utilizing Technologies with Teamwork

Technology has historically and increasingly played a pivotal role in marketing. For example, because innovations in air transportation made buyers and sellers more physically accessible, this provided a catalyst for changing how many interorganizational exchanges occur. Correspondingly, although a number of other advances have similarly impacted the buyer-seller paradigm, the recent growth of information technology (IT) has rewritten standards for how marketers manage information (Bloom, Milne, and Adler 1994), expanding opportunities for marketers to utilize this evolution strategically. For example, the increased ability to manipulate volumes of customer data allows marketers to identify and act on marketplace trends. Not surprisingly, therefore, technology has realigned the business environment (for example, Bharadwaj, Varadarajan, and Fahy 1993; Good and Stone 1995; Heide and Weiss 1995), fostering recognition that its use provides strategic advantages (Bergeron and Raymond 1992; Bharadwaj, Varadarajan and Fahy 1993; McKee and Varadarajan 1995; Senn 1992).

For the industrial marketer in particular, technology plays an increasingly crucial role, as its ownership enhances two elements vital to marketing responsibilities, performance (Cespedes 1996) and competitive advantage (Apte et al. 1990; Bharadwaj, Varadarajan and Fahy 1993; Frankwick et al. 1994; Good and Stone 1995). However, the precise framework of these advantages remains ill defined, leaving questions concerning how IT can be effectively shaped and intertwined with other evolving business-to-business strategies.

It is this potential that can be harvested from molding IT into the fabric of other marketing strategies that provides the foundation of this chapter. Specifically, this chapter will examine how IT can be successfully aligned with an emerging strategy that is becoming increasingly essential, the use of marketing teams (Deeter-Schmelz and Ramsey 1995) within industrial markets (Jessup and Valacich 1993). As part of this examination, the use of teams in the marketing environment will initially be discussed, followed by a demonstration of how IT can contribute to the overall success of marketing teams, as well as the implications of this integration for the marketer.

MARKETING TEAMS

Formally, a team is a group of two or more individuals collectively working toward the same goal (Provitera 1995). Depending upon the goals of the organization (Cespedes 1996; Hansen 1994), the group may be composed of individuals closely tied within organizational and functional boundaries (for example, marketing), or teams may be cross-functional (for example, marketing, accounting, and production), where individuals originate from a variety of disciplines and responsibilities (Hansen 1994).

Teams represent a strategic and formal decision to ensure proper resource support is provided a particular project (El-Ansary, Zabriskie, and Browning 1993). In this light, the individuals who compose teams typically represent organizational resources combined and aligned to accomplish a specific task or goal. Consistent with the basic contention that customers seek value (Webster 1994), marketing teams should therefore be shaped around the needs of customers (Zenger et al. 1994). Thus, the advantage of marketing teams to buyers rests on having more resources designated to work on their specific needs. Such a buyer-seller linkage is evident in a variety of strategic applications, where such firms as Westin Hotels and Resorts (Tyrer 1994), NEC Technologies (Damore 1995), Eastman Kodak Company (Cuneo 1995), Apple Computer (Hamlin 1994), and IBM (Gillooly 1994), are reporting the use of marketing teams to strengthen ties strategically between sellers and buyers.

In successful teams the individual members are not controlled, managed, or supervised. Instead, team members are led by a shared vision of the goals and purpose of the organization (Ray and Bronstein 1995). The nature of an environment where multiple individuals are collectively working toward one goal suggests involvement strengthens individual performance in a synergistic coupling of resources (Katzenbach and Smith 1993). As a result, the underlying purpose of constructing a team is to enhance existing organizational abilities through the coalescing of individuals who offer different strengths (for example, skills, interests, backgrounds) to a joint venture (Cespedes 1996).

THE ENVIRONMENT FOR MARKETING
TEAMS GROWS RICHER

When human resources are brought together, the strong competitive leverage gained (Shapiro 1987, 1988) suggests the usage of marketing teams can be a profitable strategy (Deeter-Schmelz and Ramsey 1995). This opportunity occurs in an environment where buyers' expectations of sellers are escalating, and marketers are faced with the challenge of differentiating and extending the utility of their products (Webster 1994). Further, the needs of buyers are increasingly becoming complex, requiring buyers and sellers to have the ability to exchange information rapidly. Consequently, marketing teams as a competitive advantage are now being widely reported in both the business (for example, Cuneo 1995; Krajewski 1994; Lucas 1994) and academic press (for example, Cespedes 1996; Olson, Walker, and Ruekert 1995). The extensive use of marketing teams as an efficient, low cost strategy (El-Ansary, Zabriskie, and Browning 1993) demonstrates expensive resources (that is, employees) can be collectively directed in harmony to mutually important organizational goals of buyers and sellers. Such versatility suggests marketers may become more seamless across organizational boundaries (Prabhaker, Goldhar and Lei 1995) as they expand marketing teams to include personnel from a variety of internal (for example, finance, accounting, and production), and external (for example, customers) sources.

Within business-to-business markets, however, opportunities are particularly bright for the future use of marketing teams because of the nature of these markets. For example, industrial markets typically require high investments to make exchanges, extended time to complete transactions, a large number of individuals involved in decisions, highly competitive markets, the need for close relationships between principal decision makers (buyers and sellers), and increasingly complex and intertwined financial attachments involving both buyers and sellers. Because of the complexity of these marketplace arrangements, therefore, the usage of marketing teams within markets will increasingly prevail. Current examples of how the use of marketing teams has expanded in markets are illustrated through the widely accepted practices of using cross functional and national account teams to work with large buyers.

The commingling of IT and the usage of marketing teams is offered as one method of enriching organizational performance. This opportunity exists because the underlying premise of team effectiveness relies on the inclusion of multiple individuals imputing knowledge (information) to a single strategy (El-Ansary, Zabriskie, and Browning 1993), and correspondingly, the role of IT is to deliver knowledge (information) to the user (Bloom, Milne, and Adler 1994; Good and Stone 1995). As such, information is the common crucial element that collectively directs marketing team activities and defines the difference between high and low marketing performance. Further, this commingling is also possible because of the barriers inherent to effective teams and the subsequent impact IT has on these barriers.

BARRIERS TO EFFECTIVE TEAMS

Because the ability of the group to communicate effectively often dictates success or failure (Varney 1989), the role of information exchange in a team setting assumes a more complex framework than simpler communication channels involving only two discrete parties (for example, a single source and receiver). The level of communication complexity escalates because of the processes required to secure information relevant to the particular objective or assignment. In simple two party interactions (see, for example, the left side of Figure 2.1) the communication processes are typically less intricate than those in teams because opportunities for problems (for example, lost, misdirected, or miscommunicated information) are minimized as the number of communication points (senders-receivers) are reduced.

As can be noted in the right side of Figure 2.1, the process of communication is inherently more complex as intragroup interaction escalates. Thus, while the use of multiple member teams provides many benefits, the inherent dynamics of teams create interaction obstacles (size, proximity of members, boundary management, cost, member empowerment, organizational support, performance assessment and accountability, complex membership, and getting people to work together) that frequently limit productivity (Monaghan 1995; Parker 1994). These barriers to team effectiveness revolve around basic interaction problems depicted in Figure 2.1 and are compatible with the key role that communication plays in the success of failure of teams (Mikalachki 1994; Reiste and Hubrich 1995). Consequently, the composition of teams (Cespedes 1996) as well

FIGURE 2.1
Comparison of Individual and Team Communication Flows

Two Individual Flow

Team Flow (Multiple Members)

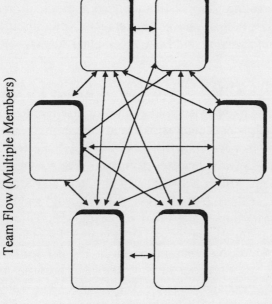

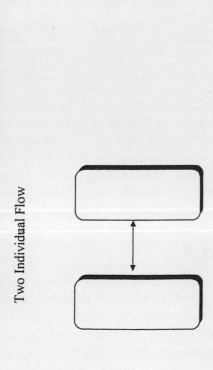

Two party communication
flow *limits* opportunities
for interaction problems

Multiple member communication
flow *increases* opportunities
for interaction problems

Source: David J. Good and Roberta J. Schultz (1997), "Technological Teaming as a Marketing Strategy," *Industrial Marketing Management,* 26 (September), 415.

as physical, psychological, and responsibility barriers all may interfere with group communication, and in turn, team performance.

Given these barriers, can a marketer strategically use teams while being consistent with the evolution, sophistication, and abilities of contemporary organizations? It is in this framework that this chapter discusses how the coupling of marketing teams and IT can be strategically advantageous.

INFORMATION TECHNOLOGY

The ongoing development of technology has enriched abilities to manage information, which is becoming significantly more important to marketers. As the need to manage knowledge has increased, this has fostered IT as the hardware or software that stores, transmits, or transforms information rapidly (Bloom, Milne, and Adler 1994; Good and Stone 1995). For example, computer links, e-mail, video conferencing, and computerized data bases (for example, statistical packages, reports, and stored information), are common examples of IT being used by industrial marketers. In this framework, the emerging power of IT rests with its ability to impact individual, organizational, and marketplace performance (Bergeron and Raymond 1992; Bharadwaj, Varadarajan, and Fahy 1993; DeLone and McLean 1992; O'Callaghan, Kaufmann, and Konsynski 1992; Thorn, Guynes, and Guynes 1990).

Although marketers are increasingly positive about the strategic use of technology (Bloom, Milne, and Adler 1994; Frankwick et al. 1994; Heide and Weiss 1995), "most modern organizations are using the hard technology of the next century with the human resource technology of the last century" (Ray and Bronstein 1995, p. 21). To this end, IT should be seen as a mechanism that enhances productivity consistent with contemporary organizational strategic activities. Compatible with this perspective, the basis of successful IT is to improve customer linkages (Gattuso 1994). Correspondingly, because marketing teams should be molded around client needs (Zenger et al. 1995) opportunities exist to integrate these strategies through technological teaming.

TECHNOLOGICAL TEAMING

Escalating opportunities for marketers to work in conjunction with other personnel (Olson, Walker, and Ruekert 1995) provide fertile situations for joint contributors (team members) to work on shared objectives (Tjosvold and Tjosvold 1993). However, as previously noted, basic barriers in communications and interaction can engulf teams, limiting productivity. To challenge these restrictions, the integration of technology and marketing teams can provide a useful strategic avenue that is consistent with the role of teams and how IT has redefined the nature of marketing interaction and communication (Stone and Good 1995).

Technological teaming refers to the use of IT to link individuals and organizations working as a cohesive team. Its underlying goal, therefore, is to use IT and marketing teams jointly and strategically to develop close customer ties. Thus, although the nature and composition of teams and technology can change, it is the impact that both collectively have on the marketer that encourages organizations to group efforts technologically. In turn, this strategic coalescing should produce beneficial outcomes for the buyer and seller. For example, when the seller is able to offer such meaningful benefits to the buyer, this is also translated into long term benefits for the seller through the ownership of a competitive advantage. Additionally, such an alliance also increases the probability that buying and selling organizations will become interconnected long term in a close relationship.

Technological teaming blends the innovative nature of teams (Petersen and Hillkirk 1991; Tubbs 1988) with the emerging capabilities and strategic use of IT. This approach, therefore, combines IT, team efforts and goals, and a client orientation. In a demonstration of how such a unification can increase productivity, Exxon Chemical Company utilized an electronic network (Exnet) to increase the availability of information to organizational members, while reducing the effort needed to share knowledge. Consequently, although the individual employees using this information system worked in a variety of locations and time zones, Exxon was able to link electronically a large variety of employees who shared common needs (Opper and Fersko-Weiss 1992).

However, in contrast to the internal example noted above, technological teaming also allows the marketer to expand externally the limits of the marketing group to include the customer. For example, buyers can be included throughout the selling cycle via e-mail to communicate daily with other marketing team members about a variety of issues, such as product specifications and installation, delivery schedules, key impending events, and so forth. In this example, the seller can be notified electronically when product inventories are near reorder points (in an ideal situation, this information might come from a variety of sources, such as warehouse and inventory records). In turn, the marketer can use this knowledge to trigger automatically a reorder with this customer, reducing opportunities to avoid selling disruptions (for example, a reassessment of all potential vendors) in highly competitive business-to-business markets.

These increased connections among team members, therefore, improve group coordination, minimize time between exchanges, and reduce opportunities for communication errors. In joint teaming of this nature, buyers and sellers can seek timely information by convening an electronic meeting composed of team members with direct responsibility for issues of interest (product quality control, finance, distribution, packaging, and so forth). Consequently, as in situations where a team's focus is external and is enhanced with direct communication between organizations on an ongoing basis, the mechanics of IT can enhance and facilitate these connections. Thus, although customers who require detailed information and coordinating mechanisms have found satisfaction working with marketing teams (Cespedes 1996), marketers who either need to systematically interchange information with clients or those who must exchange large volumes of data, IT can be a crucial tool that can provide significant competitive advantages.

WHY TECHNOLOGICAL TEAMING WORKS

The basic premise in linking information systems with marketing teams rests with the rationale that jointly embracing both entities produces positive performance results (Czajkiewicz and Wielicki 1994; Norman 1995). In a more specific sense, the performance of teams increases as the interaction quality escalates (Cespedes 1996). Correspondingly, given that a basic role of IT is to communicate accurate information rapidly, and marketing teams represent multiple parties collectively collaborating on a joint project, opportunities exist for positive linkages between the use of IT and marketing teams. For instance, a Dallas shopping center developed a marketing team to collect customer information at different retail locations for an electronic data base. The marketing team is provided valuable data (for example, marital status, income, homeowner status) by customers, which are then used by the team to expand their understanding of buyers (Gattuso 1994). IT can ensure valued information is transmitted to marketing team members in a timely fashion. The focus of merging IT and teams in this environment, of course, places a premium on working with buyers closely.

Importantly, team interaction occurs through the development of common goals of group members and the sharing of responsibilities, which in turn creates a synergistic output that should exceed individual production. The initial goal of successful IT in the team setting is, therefore, to enrich the elements of interaction and sharing. From this perspective and congruent with the marketing environment it is evident the long term goal of integrating technology and teams should be consistent with the need to improve "the effectiveness of intelligence development and decision making" (Jessup and Valacich 1993, p. 258). For example, although the traditional method of conducting meetings is dependent upon the availability of the participants, IT changes the definition of availability, removing physical presence and only requiring access to IT (for example, video conferencing). As a result, the impact of IT is to broaden the definition of managers able to engage in decision-making activities.

Based on the basic communicative nature of IT (Bloom, Milne, and Adler 1994; Good and Stone 1995), it is important to identify whether the barriers of teams can be sufficiently minimized through its use. For instance, although many firms are utilizing larger marketing teams (for example, national account and cross-functional teams) to sell products, as these teams increase in size, difficulties in communications will escalate (coordinating meeting times, arranging the availability of key personnel, and so forth). Through IT, however, it is possible for large team membership situations not to impact productivity unduly through the efficiencies of communication enabled by electronic linking. Texaco, for example, is able to use IT to support team activities across different business units (DeSanctis and Jackson 1994), underscoring its power in coordinating diverse personnel and activities.

Other common barriers that limit team productivity (for example, physical proximity and empowerment) relevant to marketers, and how IT positively impacts these restrictions are identified in Table 2.1.

Although marketing teams engage in a variety of behaviors, communication is a factor that primarily governs their success (Varney 1989). In conjunction with its ability to improve communication (Stone and Good 1995), the usage of IT offers many positive impacts on marketing teams delineated in Table 2.1. The support and rationale for technology enrichment of teams occurs because communications are positively impacted by the actual technology, as well as the improved processes created by the technology (Jessup and Valacich 1993).

Although the impacts of IT on marketing teams (in Table 2.1) are far-reaching, the issue of boundary management is of particular interest because of the emphasis many marketers are currently placing on developing and maintaining relationships with buyers. A distinctive advantage of IT is that it essentially can reduce or remove obstructions that limit access to other individuals. Hence, boundaries between personnel are reduced both within and between organizations. More specifically, communication becomes increasingly burdensome as team members are added as sending and receiving points (even when the same organizational

TABLE 2.1
Impact of Information Technology on Marketing Teams

Team Size — enhances potential number of individuals included on project; improves speed, quality, and quantity of communication flow to multiple parties (team members)

Physical Proximity — only restricted by availability of electronic contact, physical contact not required; time of contact does not have to be coordinated

Boundary Management — information technology can be set up to penetrate any organization, management level, or function; allows direct access whle not requiring physical contact or accessibility

Expensive to Operate — high initial investment, costs spread over firm, improves productivity, may reduce other costs (less than telephone, reduces travel requirements, and so forth)

Lack of Empowerment — lines of authority not impacted, restriction or access to levels of usage can empower users

Require Special Support — support needed from information technology personnel to ensure functional equipment, software, and so forth

Individual Performance Assessment — records of intrateam communication ensure tracking responsibilities; storage of team and individual data ensures proper assessment of accomplishments

Complex Membership — allows contact with any authoried personnel (for example, upper management)

Difficult to Hold Individuals and Team Accountable — all team and individual contacts electronically tracked, ensuring accountability recorded

Difficulties in Having More People Work Together — enhances intrateam communication (especially larger groups), does not restrict linkages with smaller members, improves speed and quality of communication

---

Source: David J. Good and Roberta J. Schultz (1997), "Technological Teaming as a Marketing Strategy," *Industrial Marketing Management*, 26 (September), 418.

culture is shared among team members). As cultures become more diverse, however, such as when personnel from different organizations are communicating (for example, buyers and sellers), opportunities for static between senders and receivers escalate, reducing the effectiveness of the communication.

Through technological teaming, however, such obstacles can be rapidly and effectively diffused. For example, when a buyer must swiftly communicate changing needs to a seller, there is no need to spend precious time and resources trying physically to contact (for example, telephone, mail) the appropriate person (or people) charged with this responsibility.

Instead, through technological teaming (such as e-mail), the buyer is linked electronically with the entire team assigned the responsibility of working with this account. In this setting, the buyer can almost instantly electronically contact his or her marketing team (whether it is a single person or many people) and notify appropriate individuals of the changing status. Through this approach, there is an extension of product value, as the selling team can be more inclusive and responsive to the needs of the buyer. Additionally, the needs of the buyer are better met through the ability of the seller to respond quickly to changing conditions.

The impact of IT on marketing teams fosters a number of interesting implications for the team members, management (the organization), and the recipient of the team behavior (for example, customer). Accordingly, implications of technological teaming are discussed in the following section.

STRATEGIC IMPLICATIONS

Despite the many advantages empowered by IT, these advancements have not always been embraced by marketers (Dyer 1987; Goslar 1987; Kurtz and Boone 1987; Steinberg and Plank 1987). Consequently, it should not be assumed that IT will be automatically and enthusiastically consumed by marketing teams. In fact, because the environmental influences of technology usage are strong (Raymond 1990; Turnipseed, Burns, and Hodges 1991), the integration of teams with IT requires a strong commitment on the part of the supporting organization(s). As such, upper management plays a crucial role in integrating IT within the organization (Benton and Gray 1993; Guimaraes, Igbaria, and Lu 1992; Hartman et al. 1995; Yoon, Guimaraes, and O'Neal 1995), indicating its use by marketing teams will be dictated by the willingness of management to accept technology in this role. This integration can be organizationally encouraged through endorsements and participation (for example, training of personnel, availability of the technology, technical support) in linking the task, the marketing team, and the resource support of the team. In contrast, however, when management does not actively seek to integrate marketing teams and technology, it is unlikely this assimilation will occur.

The basic contention for marketers using technological teaming originates from the value it offers buyers and sellers within these markets. Although this value can be found in many places, improved relationships between buyers and sellers represent a particularly useful and desired outcome of technological teaming. For instance, the capabilities provided by IT enhance the abilities of all team members to assess and act on a variety of situations (trends, problem areas, and so forth) that are equally important to the buyer and seller. Additionally, the nature of this integration (that is, the availability of computers for buyers and sellers that are easily linked) encourages the inclusion of the client as part of the team, which in turn more closely ties together and enriches relationships between buyers and sellers. This value is illustrated when a manufacturer requires several commodity products provided by different firms (that is, several different firms and their subsidiaries each can provide the products needed). If one seller is able to link electronically the manufacturer with a marketing team (that is, composed subsidiary members) to monitor systematically buyer inventory levels, this can be used to ensure this sellers' products are available as needed. Hence, the ability to track and predict buyer needs, even with commodity products, closely links buyers and sellers, creating a host of opportunities to cultivate strong relationships.

ORGANIZATIONAL IMPLICATIONS

Organizations that accept the strategic use of teams should also accept the necessity to integrate IT with group efforts. Basic increases in employee empowerment and responsibilities that accompany the use of teams require a significant escalation in the availability of information (which is typically made accessible through IT). In this light, it is likely that teams without the availability of IT may in fact be compelled to construct this type of mechanism to deliver the necessary information (Manz and Sims 1993). Under these conditions, it is reasonable to conclude that because the availability of technology is a key issue (Manz and Sims 1993), the success of teams may escalate at the rate at which IT is able to become organizationally intertwined. Understandably, firms that have not yet widely accepted IT (for example, computerization), may find it difficult to insert this technology selectively into a marketing team effort. For instance, business-to-business marketers who have avoided computerizing client information and who have hired salespeople who dislike using computers will find the conversion to utilizing IT a difficult challenge because of the need to change the marketing personnel, the organizational culture, and the technology.

It is also important that organizations and managers be able to adjust to changes in IT. As improvements are made, marketing teams need to revisit how these developments impact the operation of the team and in turn the client. Hence, the need exists constantly to track and assess available and applicable technology. In this vein, careful decisions need to be made that reflect the continued importance placed on using technology to link the buyer with the seller more closely and in turn not allow technology to impede, distance, or take the place of key relational associations between clients and sellers that are so important within markets.

MANAGERIAL IMPLICATIONS

The importance of the individual with respect to implementing IT within teams also has several important managerial implications (Davis, Bagozzi, and Warshaw 1992; Hays 1994). First, when a marketing team will be using technology teaming, it will be prudent to employ user friendly information technologies, coupled with generous training sessions for those individuals lacking these skills and knowledge. If this is not possible, then the marketer is faced with the additional economic challenge of having to employ or to include intentionally in its team membership those individuals professionally suited and predisposed to this task. In any case, because teams frequently are composed of individuals with different backgrounds, experiences, and skills, it will be frequently necessary to devote resources sufficient to allow each member to become comfortable using IT in the context of the group assignment. For instance, although the use of IT to enrich team performance is consistent with the expectation that future managers will be jointly comfortable with using teams and current technology (Kiechel 1994; O'Reilly 1994), managers must also be able to supervise IT effectively as well as understand how it can be best used. For example, Texaco's application of IT to promote teams among business units (DeSanctis and Jackson 1994) underscores the individual and organizational commitments required before IT and team-based activities can be integrated.

As the environment becomes more complex, the integration of IT and marketing teams will become more intense, requiring firms to structure organizational practices around team efforts (Stokes 1995). In the business-to-business environment, managers need to assess how these elements can be cohesively linked (for example, under what conditions their marketing teams most effectively use IT) and what resources are needed to support this approach. For instance, it has been recently noted that team composition is becoming more global in nature, profiting from the synergy of participants from a wide range of experiences (Solomon 1995). Consequently, firms such as Xerox, Motorola, and AT&T are now incorporating IT into team collaboration vehicles, where team member interchange is made more effective via a variety of information technologies (for example, video conferencing) that can bring the group together (Jessup and Valacich 1993). Accordingly, the advent of IT coupled with markets encourages intercultural collaboration often necessary in business-to-business markets.

FUTURE ROLE OF TECHNOLOGY
AND MARKETING TEAMS

The future role of technology and marketing teams involves gaining a better view of the individual qualities that link marketers and the technology they are comfortable with and willing to use in team situations. For example, this could involve defining the relationship between the environment (types of firms, competitors, customers, and so forth), the marketing team (size, membership composite, and so forth), and the technology selected (video conferencing, e-mail, fax, and so forth). In this vein, it would be desirable to assess if certain types of buyers prefer particular technologies and if so under what conditions. For example, there is the need to evaluate what types of information technologies assist salespeople, sales managers, marketing managers, and so forth, in the accomplishment of team and individual goals. From this basis, it can be determined if there are inconsistencies in these needs, and how selling can help organizations economically satisfy these different constituencies.

There is also a need to understand the conditions of use customers are willing to accept (for example, to what degree they are willing to be tied to a network with a seller), and to what degree sellers will have to go to accommodate technology by their clients. For example, will marketing teams have to pay for IT for some customers, or will customers view these expenditures as long-term financial and relational investments? The use of marketing teams within the framework of IT also raises questions as to what degree this technology can be used to supplant human contact. More specifically, under what particular conditions can technology teaming be substituted for the personal contact of salespeople?

The discussion presented in this chapter is designed to provide a starting point for understanding how information technologies and marketing teams can be strategically combined.

NOTE

Portions of this chapter were reprinted from *Industrial Marketing Management*, 26, 1997, "Technological Teaming as a Marketing Strategy," by David J. Good and Roberta J. Schultz, pp. 413–22, with permission from Elsevier Science.

3

Managing the
Change of Technology

In our rush to incorporate new technologies, are we forgetting a thing or three? If one word were to be used to describe technology, it may well be "change." That is, unlike other organizational tools, technology is constantly changing. In a continuum of business tools, few have experienced the number and degree of changes experienced by technology. Accordingly, technology is an ever-changing ingredient that is hard to predict. Along with this constant status of change, managers are offered conditions under which they must determine the value in making internal adjustments. In another context, change and acceptance are separate issues. Hence, management must first determine if change is appropriate, and then the decision must be made as to the strategies utilized to induce organizational change. Thus, although the scope of changes may vary, it is clear that maintaining a technological sound base requires a constant managerial, organizational, and individual willingness to adjust. In such an environment, a firm whose mission is to be in a technologically leadership position understands that the failure to change brings stable, predictable activities. Of course, constructing organizational (internal and external) technological strategies on a basis of little change increases the risk of being outdated, out-planned, and damaged. In contrast, embracing change enriches opportunities, and expands the vision of the firm and the individual. However, embracing change is accompanied by the risk of making poor adoption decisions that can foster significant impacts.

Underscoring the utilization of technologies, managers and organizations must be willing and able to adapt to a variety of environmental conditions. It is impossible to implement new advancements within an organization, particularly in the technology domain, where changes are frequent and immense, if firm adaptability is lacking. Focusing on this issue, this chapter addresses how organizations can prepare for change and accept it when presented with significant environmental transformations. In this context, this chapter also discusses how managers can recognize qualities that will help them understand the nature of such change. Most critical to dealing with change in the technology domain is how technology is viewed within the firm. In a variation of existing perspectives, therefore, we propose that linking technology to how services are visualized is a critical element in accepting change as a strategic decision.

STRATEGIC DECISION: THE ACCEPTANCE OF TECHNOLOGY TO SERVICE

Part of the problem with incorporating technology into marketing is that many businesses and managers view technology as a good and not as a service. In a fundamental examination of the difference between these elements, goods basically represent physical offerings, while services are mostly intangible (Churchill and Peter 1995). For instance, a car, baseball bat, telephone, and desk all would be considered goods. In contrast, however, services often represent less clear physical offerings (more intangible). For example, although an airline flight offers clients a physical component (an airplane), the majority of the product offering is the intangible delivery nature (the service) of this product. In similar couplings, a night at a hotel, surgery, cutting grass, bank offerings, and postal delivery all represent components of services that have a high degree of intangibility, although the intangibility is at times closely intertwined into some physical offering. Hence, although there are other traits that have been proposed at different times to be part of a service, the intangibility issue continues to represent the key separation between goods and services.

Importantly, therefore, understanding how goods and services are seen provides a key to comprehending change as it relates to technology. Hence, underscoring the role that change plays in accepting and adopting new technologies requires an understanding of the intangible nature of technology. That is, simply viewing the intangible nature of technology (the service component) as a physical offering hinders the ability of many organizations to make internal changes driven by technology, even when they are necessary.

THE EVOLUTION OF TECHNOLOGY
AS A GOOD TO A SERVICE

Logically technologies have evolved in most situations, companies, and conditions as a good, or a physical offering. An examination of technologies in most businesses suggest that they were first introduced and later controlled to a large extent by internal technicians or technically oriented personnel. The rationale behind this evolution, of course, can be seen in the complex nature of these products and the limited number of personnel who understood their operational abilities. That is, some physical instrument has always driven technology, tool, or body (computers, software, and so forth), which in turn has limited the number of users of the technology who understand its internal workings. Instead, most users of technology, particularly in recent years, have correctly focused on the benefits of the technology and not its technical aspects.

However, historically to manage technology has required in essence the ability physically to oversee manipulations in the instrument, tool, or body. Of course, such overseeing has typically been done by this person often referred to as a technician. Not surprisingly, from an inspection of the technicians that we have known and in contrast to the reason that the technology was secured, most of these individuals (technicians) see themselves as overseeing the physical product and not the benefits that the technical product provides. The reasons for this perspective are varied, although it is critical to note that technicians are specialists in how they manage a particular product and not the services they offer.

Thus, from these early days technology has been seen as a good (a physical entity) and not as a service. Today that outlook generally remains the same as the nature of technicians has resulted in these individuals widely influencing others to see technology in the context of the physical product that delivers the technology and not the benefits it provides. For instance, most technicians see computers (the physical good) as the primary offering of information technology. Compare this outlook to an accountant who sees the benefits of computerization but has little concern for the actual computer. Not surprisingly, the role and influence that technicians have played in the integration of technology throughout most businesses has become an attitude that has permeated most firms.

In contrast to this outlook, consider that technology is really a serv-ice. That is, the offerings of technology to users are not a physical product but a service. The benefits under this outlook become the chief tool to be managed. In turn, when improvements need to be made, they are made under the vision of "what benefits will be created," and not "what changes I must make." Of course, under this scenario the role of technology is not to enhance some physical product but to enrich the abilities of those who use the technology, as the enrichment becomes a service.

THE ORGANIZATION: MANAGING THE CHANGE OF TECHNOLOGY

With little doubt, changes in technology are frequent and often dramatic. Consider, for example, the rapidness in which personal computers overtook the corporate world. Grasping the short time period in which typewriters went from mainstay tool to afterthought is staggering. In this environment, those who use technology must comprehend that the offering of technology is much like standing at the beachfront. No matter how the environmental conditions change, the water keeps coming in. Sometimes from wave to wave there are slight differences, yet the waves never cease and the changes are not always predictable. Comparable to the context of the technology framework, changes in this environment are sometimes small and sometimes quite large. Most importantly, changes are inevitable and never ending. To be successful in this setting, managers must develop a plan for dealing with the change of technologies. That is, because of the constant evolution of technologies, firms that are leaders in technology will develop plans for being able to manage the changes in technology. In this context, understanding the relationship of technology as a service enhances the probability of being able to manage the change.

The premise of this chapter is that seeing technology as a service and not a good is key to managing the change of technology. That is, given the rapid evolution of most technologies, it is critical to be mobile, retaining the ability to deviate from previously established patterns of investments and behaviors and not to be tied to physical offerings. For instance, when changes are made to physical products (for example, automobiles), this can initially be a time-consuming process because changes must be made to the structure of the product. Over time, however, when such changes are made to physical products, these changes are noticeable to the human eye. In turn, the education processes required to communicate the changes to individuals who are impacted (for example, salespeople), are small because people are able to individually perceptualize these modifications.

Consistent with this outlook, when technology is seen as a good this places a great deal of emphasis on the physical nature of its presence (for example, computerization). Under this perspective, seeing a physical aspect of technology focuses improvements, changes, and adjustments on making physical manipulations (for example, changes in the look of the good) that are not necessarily noticeable or important to most technology users who seek specific benefits.

In contrast, as an intangible element a service underscores technological offerings as those that emphasize the benefits of the offering. Thus, when technology is viewed as a service the focus is on users and the benefits that they engender and not on the physical properties (for example, computers) of the technology. Under this perspective, several different managerial impacts must be examined.

Intra-firm Communication

Change in this environment is driven less by dramatic technical changes (which frequently occur) and more by development in terms of the needs of users. What this outlook requires is a strong commitment on the part of management to ensure that the users have sufficient knowledge to anticipate the needs of their department and functions. In turn, these needs must be transferable (communicable) so they can be interpreted within the context of specific abilities of technologies required. Under this approach, management must be committed to ensure that employees of different groups regularly communicate their needs to technicians. Accordingly, the role of the technician in this environment is regularly to pursue organization members for the purpose of developing short- and long-term plans outlining their specific needs as they relate to technology offerings. For instance, the assignment of technicians and technology users to a committee that systematically overviews future technology needs enhances opportunities for technology being strategically implemented. In this domain, the emphasis must be the ongoing stated desired of management for such communication to occur.

Intertwining Providers and Equipment

Because of the nature of services (where others often provide them), services and service providers are frequently intertwined, making no distinction or effort to clearly separate the two. Accordingly, the technical provider must be a bridge between the technical offering and users.

Failure to have such a bridge makes it impossible to make dramatic changes in technology, because users will not be able to communicate effectively with technicians. Thus, the technicians must see themselves as service providers, who have the role of supporting the application of technology for others. To accomplish this goal, management must strategically set out to employ technicians who professionally do not see this as a contrast to their individual views. Further, management must regularly ensure that the technicians understand that their role of working with non-technicians is a critical component of their job. Hence, reward structures (for example, compensation) must be designed to support this view. Technicians who do accept this role must understand the long-term financial results of such a view.

Non-technical Jargon

Because the role of communication is extremely high when changes are made in technology, technicians and users must be able to communicate effectively with each other. In a critical consideration, technicians must be willing to communicate with users in a non-technical format. Hence, the usage and application of barriers to understanding between the two parties (technician and user) must be removed (for example, no technical language), with this responsibility usually being placed upon the technician.

Relationship between Parties

We propose that increasing the effectiveness of adapting to changes in technology should be built at least in part on the relationships that are built within the corporate community. For example, when a computer information systems manager has a poor working relationship with the human resources department, it can be difficult to get both parties to work closely when establishing the future technology needs of human resources.

In the above example, seeing technology as a service places a great deal of emphasis on the relationship of the service provider to the user group, as well as strong linkages to the field of technology. That is; as a service, the emphasis is on the provider and not just the equipment. Hence, working closely places an emphasis on the relationship between the parties. Therefore, as a primary consideration in this environment, technicians overseeing corporate technologies must serve two separate groups intimately who are inherently critical to embracing change in the service provided to technology users (technical and non-technical staffs). Consider in this context the reality of what most organizational structures encourage among employees. The infrastructure of most firms is built in such a manner that employees regularly work, communicate, and even socialize (for example, lunch) with members only of their own internal structure (that is, the same department). As a result, it is common for relationships between members of separate departments (for example, computer information systems and marketing) to have only minimal contact with other, external groups. Yet, despite the separation by location and objectives of these groups, when the need arises, we ask these individuals to work cohesively with each other, forming a strong internal synergy. Although possible in some situations, the boundaries between technical personnel and other, non-technical professionals often make building such relationships difficult if not impossible.

We propose that both parties (technical and non-technical employees), led by technical personnel should ensure that relationships are built and maintained between the separate groups. This suggests, for example, these individuals must produce the kind of effort that allows for a relationship to be constructed between different and often quite separate parties. Ensuring that such areas as trust, communication, and commitment are offered as part of the working agreements, it is necessary for relationships to be constructed that break down traditional organizational structures if we expect technicians to work cohesively with non-technical staff members. How does such cross-fertilization actually happen? It can begin with the assignment of office departments (intermixing when possible of departments and functions), the cross functional assignments of personnel, and nurturing of relationships built through mutual assignments (joint committees) and friendships (encourage cross socialization). However, it will not occur without the knowledge and direction of management.

4

Technology's Influence on
Relationships:
Internal and External

For many years the success of business ventures has relied on the ability of two parties, each with different but inter-related objectives and agendas, to construct and maintain strong attachments. Based on the premise that doing business with a partner (one who shares risk and returns) can enhance value, managers have spent a great deal of effort in recent years attempting to understand the complex relationships that can exist between two separate parties. For instance, when marketers understand that constructing and maintaining successful buyer-seller relationships provides significant strategic advantages to both parties, they can use this understanding as the basis for a selling strategy (relationship selling) as well as a resource commitment to the buying party that may last many years.

In this pursuit, buyers and sellers have spent a great deal of resources trying to understand and refine the mechanisms necessary to link through relationships. Driven by distinct needs, buyers and sellers in this environment found it necessary to balance their interactions, anticipating the benefits received, as well as exploring the strength, frequency, and duration of successful partnering interactions.

Underscoring the basic premise that relationships can foster meaningful value, business relationships are increasingly being seen as strategic. For example, although a computer seller relies on a buyer to make purchases, at the same time the buyer relies on the seller to provide and maintain the appropriate state-of-the-art technologies for the purchased system.

As a result of such an outlook, sellers and buyers must individually and collectively determine the degree to which they are willing to make long-term attachments.

Correspondingly, other business functional managers (for example, accountants and production engineers) are also now· seeking methods designed to utilize business relationships within the context of their unique responsibilities. Providing the opportunity to construct such strategic success, a great deal has been written in the academic and popular press about the emerging role that relationships play among various business partners. Including both formal and informal business structures coupled with a diversity of company situations (size, mission, location, and so forth), understanding relationships within businesses is an increasingly complex issue.

Relying strongly on the ability of two parties to give and receive value (for example, Bagozzi 1975; Kotler 1972), relationships can be hindered or valued through a variety of external influences. Although these influences include a wide array of issues (management style, employees, location of business, and so forth), the purpose of this chapter is to assess the emergence of one particularly forceful effect of technology on business relationships. As an asset of communication that has and will continue to impact dramatically the ability to form and maintain business relationships, technology will reshape the notion of business relationships both within the context of the ability to communicate and the perception of those individuals actually communicating.

In the framework of understanding the complexities of personal interactions, this chapter will discuss how interpersonal relationships can be impacted by technology. This examination will be done from both the potential in the current domain and in environments where the parameters for attachments will change.

THE STRATEGIC IMPACT OF TECHNOLOGY ON BUSINESS RELATIONSHIPS

Consider the same use of an identical technology by two different managers. In this illustration, less assertive managers can use video conferencing to contact distant employees with little concern about face-to-face confrontations. For these managers the physical distance between the individuals allows more opportunities to avoid "in your face" types of meetings that aggressive employees might employ. Accordingly, managers having this trait might use video conferencing to avoid conflict or contact with certain employees. In contrast, more assertive managers can use the same technology to hold frequent review meetings with distant employees at a reduced cost (for example, limited travel), held in conjunction with face-to-face contact. Properly presented, employees difficult to manage would see little or no difference in the style of management through video conferencing. Consequently, through the proper management of the employee and the correct utilization of the technology, little is lost in interpersonal communications. Instead, technology may more efficiently fulfill interpersonal requirements, abilities, or opportunities. As a result, there are strategic factors that must be considered when implementing technologies that relate directly to interpersonal business relationships.

Historically, although the underlying communal theme of business relationships has stressed opportunities that can be cultivated through positive alliances (for example, Anderson, Hakansson, and Johanson 1994; Anderson and Weitz 1992; Ganesan 1994; Gundlach and Murphy 1993), this condition can be complicated through technology. That is, viewed from a communication process perspective, technology can be considered as a reduction in external noise in interchange (an asset), or it can be considered as a major distraction (noise) in effective multiparty interaction.

Business attachments are built upon a number of inter-personal qualities (for example, trust, commitment, open communication), making relationships difficult to maintain under any conditions (Keefe and Maypole 1983). As the circumstances of attachment constantly change in environments that are increasingly dynamic (Baxter and Simon 1993; Montgomery 1993; Simmel 1950), it is interesting that one of the most dynamic changes that is expected to occur in the next decade is the influence of technology on this part of the business environment. In this domain, the need will continue to exist to manage attachments strategically as a form of strategic opportunity (Kramer and Grossman 1987; Wiewel and Hunter 1985), although technology will impact the manner and degree to which connections will flourish. Correspondingly, although it is clear that as business has become more sophisticated, and greater reliance is placed on the interconnections between partners, factors such as trust and commitment as part of relationships will change appearance in light of new technology.

We are, however, not proposing that the specific elements of a relationship per se will change. Those elements that define ongoing business attachments within reason will essentially continue in ongoing relationships. For instance, the role of trust, commitment, and communication should not change with the organizational advent of new technology. What will change, however, is that as we enhance our understanding of business technologies we will increasingly realize that these technologies create an environment where the interpretation of these elements and the exchange itself will change.

For instance, some industries have a long tradition of favoring good customers over less profitable ones. Credit card issuers, airlines, and mail-order companies cater to premier customers. Banks are by far the largest industry to utilize technology devices to assess the profit and loss of each customer to weed out the money losers. According to Market Line Associates, an Atlanta bank-consulting firm, the top 20 percent of typical bank customers produce a disproportionate amount of overall profit (Brooks 1999). Therefore, some firms may find alienating some customers to be profitable in order to ward off competitors from grabbing highly profitable customers. In recent years, banks have spent about $500 million on software and consultants, and the number is expected to grow to at least $500 million per year in the near future. One bank, First Union, estimates added annual revenues of $100 million as a result of new technological systems. This type of software lights up on a customer-service center computer screen by a customer's name a green, yellow, or red light, which indicates the extent to which a representative should grant waivers.

Consider a historical illustration to demonstrate the impact of technology and relationships. In this illustration conceive an employee who grew up using the telephone to interact with friends, relatives, and others. When this young man or woman entered the business world, he or she had learned to socialize via the telephone. In comparison, this employee has fostered an interactive basis that is founded on the utilization of the telephone in dealing with others, different than his or her great-grandparents who may have not have had a telephone in their home. Thus, the younger worker matured in an environment where he or she socialized with others, many of whom he or she may have never physically seen. This form of communication (telephone) fostered a host of new skills that became part of his or her life. For instance, this young person probably now routinely listens for verbal cues that are interpreted into physical assessments (for example, light voice that suggests smiling) that are regularly included as part of the communication process. From these interpretations, these assessments often are used in making life time decisions (for example, this person and I share common interests).

Thus, from the concurrent evolution of an increasingly technologically developed society and a growing importance placed on relationships, we propose two strategic implications that, depending upon the situation of the business, employees, and technology, can be used to gain a strategic advantage. Specifically, we propose that management should consider periodic assessments of three key areas that directly and indirectly influence the interaction of technology and business relationships.

Assessments of Internal and External Communications

Through a periodic assessment of how communications occur within the firm, it will be possible and in fact necessary to evaluate the degree to which relationships will be impacted via technology. That is, the question hinges on whether there will be significant or minimal impacts as technology develops. Hence, a variety of questions need to be answered within this framework. For example, this includes questions such as, are primary contacts external or internal? How do these contacts occur (in person or through another medium)? What is the length and intensity of these contacts?

How Important Are Business Relationships

The level of importance of relationships plays a role in assessing how technology will impact relationships. If relationships are less important (for example, the firm is chiefly transactional by nature), there should be less concern. In contrast, if relationships play a critical role in the success of the firm, such an investigation becomes more important. For example, in retailing, the personal interaction and relationship between the buyer and seller has historically been considered very important. As opportunities for implementing online ordering have escalated, retailers must find ways to retain these connections. In the golfing business as an illustration of this principle, buyers have historically gone to a retail shop to examine and hold products (for example, golf clubs) before making a purchase. Changing that interaction through online ordering has placed a greater burden on the retailer to enhance that relationship, or at least to prevent its demise, as the mechanisms for ordering have evolved from store front to computer top. Retailers like International Golf Outlet attempt to retain the customer relationship in this environment through their individualized e-mail responses to customer inquiries, reporting they "want long-term relationships . . . to replicate the feel of a good golf shop" (Kramer 1998, p. 87). Just as in a store, however, failing to provide quality or timely responses to customer questions allows buyers plenty of reasons to find another retailer. Therefore, a strong focus in such relationships must be on the construction of a quality exchange.

How Will Technology Change Business Relationships in the Future

Under existing conditions, a determination must be made to assess to what degree changes are expected in the existing technological and relational environment. Representing one of the most difficult challenges of managers, the goal of this vision is to anticipate strategically changing human expectations for personal interactions and to interpret how technology will interface with these relationships. Although this is quite a difficult task to accomplish, an examination of the outlook for long-term relationships is particularly critical in some businesses. For instance, if organizations that have a strong inside sales force can anticipate how emerging trends in technology will alter the face of how their sales force contacts and deals with customers, this will provide sufficient time to provide needed resource commitments. Thus, through such forecasting a system can be designed that embraces these changes and allows organizations to be prepared for marketplace alterations.

ORGANIZATIONAL IMPACTS

We see the greatest organizational impact of technology on relationships on the ability of managers to communicate via various forms of technology. More specifically, a basic tenet of a business relationship is the ability of the individuals to directly communicate with each other. In this context, the organization must create an environment where the technology does not interrupt or interfere with communications. In fact, technology should be shaped in such a fashion as to enhance communication flows, which in turn theoretically enhance business relationships. Yet, as we stated earlier, we see opportunities for technology to change (positively and negatively) the nature of organizational communications.

In this environment, the movement of communications within the firm will become increasingly more rapid and less personal. The question is, does this interrupt or enrich business relationships? Consider the usage of e-mail. With a single command, messages can be sent organizationally, regionally, nationally, or internationally. In this context, there is little question of the ability of technology to reach out and embrace users. For example, international travelers regularly utilize cell phones to keep them in constant contact with business associates, regardless of where they are traveling. Yet, the ability to contact does not ensure better communication, simply better availability. For this reason, we propose that organizations must work to ensure that employees are schooled in the processes of creating and maintaining relationships within the parameters of technology. Because we contend that technology reduces the need for personal contacts, many individuals will use this change to reduce their interaction with other professionals.

Organizations must be aware of this environment, and as such, efforts need to be constantly made to educate employees in the processes of creating and maintaining relationships. In fact, we are proposing that effective organizations will increase their formal training and education of employees in relationship building. Importantly, therefore, we propose that the role of technology will not dramatically change even as technologies evolve. Instead, people will change in terms of their interactions with technologies. Consider, for example, the advent of the telegraph, telephone, radio, teletype, fax, e-mail, and teleconferencing as examples. As each of these advancements occurred, the role of the communication did not change substantially. Instead, as the technologies changed, the users changed their usage of technology and their immediate interface with their communication partners.

In recent years the role of technology (specifically information technologies) within business firms has chiefly been to enhance communications. We do not see this changing. Instead, managers must learn to adapt employees to the conditions that are evolving technologically. The nature of successful firms will allow and drive employees to adapt to evolving technologies, utilizing these tools to enhance interpersonal communications. In contrast, less effective organizations will not consider the impacts of technology on individual interactions, and as a result, over time business relationships in these firms (inter and intra) will become increasingly less solid.

MANAGERIAL IMPACTS

From a managerial perspective, there are several specific areas that management needs to assess and act upon as they directly relate to the supervision of employees. Although in general the scope of these activities may vary (for example, based on the number of employees in a firm), management must anticipate the specific influence of technology on employees and in turn install a variety of organizational mechanisms and processes. Hence, from a managerial perspective these issues should include an understanding of the following.

Personal Skills Needed for Interpersonal Communication Have Changed

Individuals unable to master the new technological communication processes will be unable to construct business relationships that are based on or utilize in part business technologies. Incompatible to the adage that concludes, "you can't teach an old dog new tricks," there are some individuals who you can teach new technologies and some you cannot. Accordingly, the premise of this point is that first there is a need to identify those individuals who are capable of making changes in their interpersonal relationship-building processes. Second, there is a need for management to expand its understanding of personal qualities that are needed to construct business relationships.

As a primary example, consider the rapid evolution of the many Internet servers that offer chat rooms, where people can discuss a wide array of views ranging from politics, sports, entertainment, or romance to breaking news. Interestingly, many of these chatters never have met the other party (or parties) they are communicating with, remaining content to talk with an individual who 20 years ago we would have considered a stranger. Yet today, these individuals comfortably build personal and professional relationships, complete with detailed and often intimate knowledge of the other, all received from typing in words and expressing views in a monitor forum. As such, in this forum the process of building relationships has changed. We need to develop a stronger basis for identifying how relationships can be constructed via technology (for example, e-mail). In this vein, management must, therefore, be able to identify those traits that lend themselves to building strong relationships in this domain.

Businesses Must Be Prepared in the Long Term for the Nature of How Relationships Will Be Initiated

Today, many relationships are initiated through non-personal technological based contact. For instance, as "cybershopping" allows buyers to remain at their computers, ordering products such as music, videos, books, food, wine, clothes, and travel (Taylor 1998), the premise of typical retailing has changed. Increasingly, buyers, sellers, and intermediaries will initiate contact not through a personal interchange (for example, walking into the store), but instead through some less personal contact mechanism (for example, information technology, such as fax or e-mail).

Under these conditions, the parties must be prepared to enhance and develop relationships that were not formed as the result of some physical agreement or contact (for example, seeing the smile of a person). For example, the salesperson who receives contact and orders via e-mail does not have the advantage of receiving immediate nonverbal feedback (for example, nodding the head) on the product. Therefore, it will be incumbent upon the salesperson in this setting to become comfortable fostering a relationship with an individual with whom he or she has no physical contact. Often driven by factors such as distance between parties, those desiring to maintain this type of relationship must create processes that allow for the development of attachments. For example, excessive checking of the validity of the contact (for example, credit checks) must be done carefully, ensuring that activities do not restrict opportunities for the relationship to develop. Equally, employees must be schooled in dealing with such contacts, learning to be comfortable with these attachments (for example, "I only do business with people I've met").

Business Social Interactions in the Office Will Change

As the nature of interactions evolves, unique social collections will occur, driven by common interest and use of technologies. For example, the traditional gathering of people at the coffeepot to discuss interesting office developments will change. Although some managers will no doubt welcome this change with open arms, it will also bring other, less definitive developments. For instance, under this setting the atmosphere will surely be modified, providing more limitations on the opportunities for interoffice friendships, and the associated benefits such closeness brings will be reduced.

Instead, individuals will be included in shared e-mail groups, passing information throughout the firm electronically. Such electronic interactions will foster a uniqueness in the informal organizational hierarchy, as certain employees will become recognized for their informal power (just as before) acquired through technology skills.

Correspondingly, some employees will be excluded from informal organizational charts because of their inability to manage these technology skills that enhance communication between firm members. As a result, employees wishing to become part of the "in group" must acquire the technology communication skills of the majority and be willing, systematic users of these tools.

Managers Must Be Able to Identify These Individuals Who Are Skilled at Technological Relationships and Place Them in a Role Where Their Skills Can Best Be Utilized

It is our belief that just as some individuals are more skilled at making a strong interpersonal impact at first meeting, there are individuals who are more skilled at constructing and maintaining relationships via technology. For instance, because some people are more skilled at writing effective letters, they are often placed in positions where such correspondence is required. Consistent with this observation and as the business domain increasingly relies on technology to enhance business contacts, the need will grow to maintain such interconnections despite a different medium. Consider the salesperson who only deals via Internet and phone with customers and he or she can construct a sense of trust from the customer. Obviously this salesperson will strategically be in an advantageous position for the firm. Equally, management must accept that some individuals will be less skilled at this endeavor, suggesting the need to place distance between them and the technology. Also, some positions (auditors, customer service representatives, technical sales support salespeople, and so forth), may not be in a position where they can avoid the interaction between technology and interpersonal relationships.

5

Entrepreneurs and Technology

Entrepreneurs within business markets increasingly create the potential for enriched productivity through exploration into untapped markets. The growing interest in an entrepreneurial vision as a driving organizational force can be illustrated through the significant amount of attention contemporary practitioners give this subject, as well as the large number of academic entrepreneurial programs that have developed in recent years. Business magazines are filled with stories about successful entrepreneurs. However, despite the attention given to the entrepreneurial philosophy, this outlook does not come risk free. The willingness to be an entrepreneur also generates considerable opportunities for failure. For instance, although personal computers have certainly been a successful venture for many individuals and organizations, there have also been many hardware and software firm failures.

Entrepreneurial opportunities are particularly useful when individuals and organizations are able to explore and expand the needs of a marketplace. That is, entrepreneurs are most successful when they are able to find and exploit a marketplace niche. For instance, being able to perform effectively a variety of computing functions at an economically manageable cost played a critical role in the development and placement of personal computers within business communities. It is within this context that the basis of this chapter is formed. Specifically, this chapter will discuss how the interaction of technology and entrepreneurs can be successfully utilized strategically. Consider in this context Tom Cannon (Goddard 1997), who has proposed that we are about to enter a third industrial revolution. Driven by factors such as technology and entrepreneurship, the evidence demonstrates that it will become increasingly critical for firms to merge this evolving atmosphere because of the differences these outlooks often require. Such blending, however, is possible when accompanied and driven by a unique individual. In this framework, this chapter will address the importance and role of this person in an emerging marketplace. We will also identify critical trends that embrace both concepts (technology and entrepreneurial perspectives), noting that successful business firms benefit when they are able to employ individuals who embrace both technological and entrepreneurial worlds.

To meet these objectives, we will initially discuss entrepreneurs and the environment in which they operate. Entrepreneurial perspectives will then be discussed in the technological environment as a strategic choice that fosters both risks and rewards. From this, readers then will be able to design a strategic approach to identifying and employing a key individual for the next decade, the technological entrepreneur.

THE TECHNOLOGICAL ENTREPRENEUR

The role of innovators within modern business structures cannot be overlooked, as the introduction of ideas and products has increasingly become a basis for enhanced productivity. Although a number of reasons are often offered for one becoming an entrepreneur, from an organizational perspective it is the ability to increase output that often offers the primary motivation for encouraging such an outlook among employees. Although firms typically endorse this type of behavior, it is not a function solely of the beliefs and attitudes of the individual. Instead, the individual becomes an entrepreneur as a result of individual, organizational, and environmental conditions that are synthesized in the work setting. Accordingly, the concept of being entrepreneurial is becoming more visible (Carland, Hoy, and Carland 1988), as contemporary revelations suggest that the nature of entrepreneurship offers increasingly attractive rewards for its successful planned application within certain organizations.

Incorporating a wide spectrum of deployments from the management of data (Koreto 1996) to developing improved knowledge of markets (Pillsbury 1997), the parallels in entrepreneurship philosophies and the development of technology suggest the potential of significant benefits for those who use technology to cultivate an entrepreneurial opportunity.

For example, if a sales manager is able to utilize an expert system to create accurate sales forecasts and quota assignments, this not only frees his or her time for other important activities (for example, coaching of salespeople), but the construction and utilization of such data bases provide a number of other long-term benefits (for example, accurate representation of potential compensation from a territory, lower turnover if salespeople believe the forecasts are accurate, long-term organizational forecasting). Importantly, however, and despite the advantages this approach may offer, not all individuals are suited to merging technology and innovation.

Critical to understanding the intersection of entrepreneurs and technology is an understanding of what an entrepreneur really is, and what makes this individual different. Typically, an entrepreneur engages in a particular kind of act and is willing to engage in risk and innovation for the potential of gathering additional opportunities (Churchill and Muzyka 1994; Stearns and Hills 1996). Being entrepreneurial, therefore, involves a number of characteristics, such as innovativeness, autonomy, risk taking, competitive aggressiveness, and proactiveness. These individual traits are subsequently influenced by organizational (size, structure, strategy) and environmental (external) factors (Lumpkin and Dess 1996). For instance, an individual might be an entrepreneur, but her organization's physical size (for example, very large) restricts entrepreneurial activities because the structure of the firm reduces her ability to make innovative decisions. Being an entrepreneur is a complex combination of conditions, involving a host of managerial issues (Matthews, Quin, and Franklin 1996) reflective of the firm's willingness to engage in proactive innovations and risks (Miller 1983).

Entrepreneurs have historically been viewed as those who invent products (telephones, personal computers, and so forth), and not necessarily those who invent applications. However, in a significant change from this traditional perspective, businesses have increasingly begun to recognize that both of these individuals (the inventor of products and the inventor of ideas) are entrepreneurs in a similar context who create substantial organizational value. In fact, because the innovation of ideas is less expensive and more easily accomplished, the individual who performs the former task may be a more valued asset than the creator of products. This viewpoint is critical because most organizations rely somewhat on products and to a greater extent on people, suggesting that being an entrepreneur of ideas in contemporary business organizations is at least as important as being a product innovator. For example, if an accountant is able to use computer technology to report more rapidly actual costs of product sales, this discovery can be worth a great deal to his or her firm.

Accepting that the unique discovery (and application) of ideas represents an entrepreneurial activity allows business organizations to offer the potential for development and growth outside of the stereotype people often have of entrepreneurs. In turn, the firm enlarges the opportunity for entrepreneurial ideas to prosper and cultivate organizationally under this perspective. From this basis, it is important to understand the entrepreneur's organization as well as the individual entrepreneur, since by understanding this vision the technological entrepreneur can be more closely examined.

ORGANIZATIONAL IMPACTS

Despite their potential benefits, business organizations are consistent in their underlying desire either to seek or avoid entrepreneurial activities (Morris and Sexton 1996). Correspondingly, not every organization can necessarily utilize technology or desires to enrich their entrepreneurial offerings through such advances.

Firms that have not yet made the decision or have failed to implement the necessary organizational structures required of a successful entrepreneurial effort will find integrating technology with an entrepreneurial perspective offers a difficult challenge. Typically, firms will most likely not be able to use technology to drive the organization to an entrepreneurial vision. Instead, technology and entrepreneurship must be carefully and strategically blended, as managers seek an organizational balance where both entrepreneurial attitudes and a technological vision are encouraged to prosper collectively, creating a synergistic effect. For example, if employees are not persuaded to discover new methods of applying video conferencing to a unique marketplace, it is unlikely that employees will exert significant effort in this endeavor. To develop this blending, the organization (and top management) must communicate clearly that it is appropriate for employees to seek innovative methods, applications, uses, and opportunities to integrate technology into the firm. For example, if compensation is tied to entrepreneurial technological innovation, it is more likely to occur. Underscoring this emphasis, if the organization fails to acknowledge or encourage this condition, it will not occur. Further, the greater the technological limitations placed on employees (for example, not making contemporary technologies available), the fewer chances exist to integrate these philosophies. Consequently, employing and deploying technological entrepreneurials is a strategic organizational investment choice that must be assessed against the costs of this approach.

STRATEGIC IMPACTS

The Integration of Technology and the Entrepreneurial Perspective

Despite the gains of utilizing an entrepreneurial path, the risk of being unsuccessful is always a distinct and clear possibility that must be considered as part of the strategic set. That is, many organizations and individuals who seek to become entrepreneurs fail. There are no promises or guarantees that simply being or becoming an entrepreneur ensures success.

Equally, not all technology fits into all business organizations. For example, the rapid development of notebook computers has not resulted in universal acceptance, application, or benefits, despite widely documented advantages to individual users and their organizations. As a result, the combination of technology and being entrepreneurial can be a valued strategic asset or a costly venture. In this setting, management must determine both individually and collectively if technology and an entrepreneurial vision can be successfully merged in their particular organization. Based upon the traits of the firm and employees, therefore, management must be willing to accept that these components do not always fit nicely into an organization.

Because all entrepreneurs are not suited to the effective utilization of technology, this commingling is a particularly critical issue that must be resolved by top management. Correspondingly, not all technologists have the qualities (risk taking, innovativeness, and so forth) necessary to be an entrepreneur. Hence, although engaging in risky ventures certainly may enrich the ability of marketers and the firm to generate additional revenue, this choice comes with an individual and organizational price that must be weighed within the context of the cost and reward. The decision to integrate technology with entrepreneur pursuits must be examined carefully and assessed in the context of the rewards and costs that such an approach engenders each specific organization and manager. Evident in the newspapers that daily report on a large number of entrepreneurs unable to accomplish their ventures successfully, financial insolvency is an increasingly common occurrence that hinders both entrepreneurs and those engaging in technology. As a result, being an entrepreneur and utilizing technology requires a strong strategic commitment on the part of the firm.

Organizations making the decision to pursue an entrepreneurial roadway, assisted through the strategic intervention of technology, must be willing to commit significant resources to this effort. Weighed against the decision to cultivate the technological entrepreneur, organizations desiring

this approach must understand in depth the individual who is the technological entrepreneur.

The Technological Entrepreneur

The technological entrepreneur is a rare firm asset who is the product
of individual and organizational coalescing. Interestingly, however,
although such an individual produces significant opportunities, the qualities and nature of both of these individuals separately (an entrepreneur and
an individual interested in technology) may be in conflict. Demonstrated
through the qualities presented in Table 5.1, these contrasts tell us about
the challenges that face this individual and the organization in which he
or she works.

As can be seen in Table 5.1, the differences between the technologist
and entrepreneur can be quite dramatic. For instance, entrepreneurs

TABLE 5.1
Comparative Qualities of Entrepreneur and Technologist

Entrepreneur
    Risk taker
    Competitive
    Likes autonomy
    Dislikes bureaucracies
    Aggressive
    Desires to be leader
    Thinks applications
    Desires to find opportunities
    Constant belief in own correctness
Technologist
    Pays limited attention to risks, rewards, or failures
    Little interest in progress of others, self-consumed innovator
    Thinks in terms of technical progress
    Dislikes interference with pursuits
    Narrow vision beyond own tasks
    Not application oriented
    Competitive superiority not critical
    Technological superiority critical
    Assumes technology opportunities always exist
    Constant belief in own correctness

---

typically believe that under the right conditions, opportunities within markets exist. Illustrating the stark distinction that can exist between these groups, a technologist typically presumes that a market does exist for each and every technology. Other critical differences in areas such as risk taking, level of aggressiveness, and degree of application orientation of products all support the dramatic differences that frequently exist between the technologist and entrepreneur. However, it is our observation that there are some critically skilled individuals who are able to transcend these barriers that seemingly are mutually exclusive. Referred to here as the technological entrepreneur, this individual holds the key to the successful integration of technology and entrepreneur actions.

The qualities of the technological entrepreneur reflect a unique person not readily available in most organizations or available through normal employment avenues. In this sense, wanting to be entrepreneurial and being entrepreneurial represent distinct issues. Equally, wanting to be a technologist and being a technologist are not necessarily the same. Hence, it should be no surprise that many who believe they are technological entrepreneurs are not. For instance, we are reminded of the president of a large technology firm who steadfastly reminded everyone that his entrepreneurial vision would lead the firm into a new decade of growth and prosperity. As the president constantly made technical decisions that were in conflict with the recommendations of technical support personnel, the firm soon found itself in technical disarray, offering products that were not technically comparable to marketplace needs. Burdened by several years of internal conflict with technically oriented managers, the president left the firm, leaving behind managers who had been recruited as part of a new entrepreneurial vision. These remaining managers were left to work in an environment (highly technical) in which they had little or no experience, which created a history of problems (conflict over the direction of the firm, new product development, marketplaces, and so forth). Not surprisingly, the firm went through significant costly adjustments after this period to realign the firm. From this illustration, it is evident that the danger of misusing or misidentifying such an individual is likely to create negative synergy throughout the firm. Further, although these individuals appear to be more productive at higher levels in the organizational chain, the dangers of negative outcomes are also possibly enhanced at these more prominent positions.

Before seeking these individuals it is critical to ensure that the organization does have a need for such an individual. Accordingly, a list of the qualities that such an individual produces to the firm are noted in Table 5.2.

TABLE 5.2
Example Offerings of Technological Entrepreneurs

A Technological Entrepreneur can . . .
    identify early technological trends
    assess technical merits of new products
    more easily understand technical applications
    comprehend when/where/how to merge technology within markets
    work with technical and marketing personnel
    reduce tensions between critical groups (technical and marketing)
    evaluate the net cost/return of technical and marketing efforts
    broaden the vision of the firm and employees
    energize employees and the firm mission
    attract other technologists and entrepreneurs
    create meaningful long term marketing and technical strategies

---

As should be evident, sources of technological entrepreneurs are not guaranteed to produce individuals who will work effectively in every organization. Again, the importance of ensuring that such an individual will be able to fit into the structure of the employing firm must be stressed.

What This Individual Can Do

In an environment where technology and new opportunities are rapidly merging, the rewards offered individuals and their firms are growing. The key, of course, is finding the right technology to take advantage of for a particular situation. For example, and as part of an interesting paradox, successful organizations have historically (pre-1980s) been characterized as large enough to engage in certain marketplace operations. In general, many of these activities were defined as being costly, limiting the number and types of firms and managers willing to attack these markets. For instance, marketing to telephone companies was often limited to larger firms because of the resources required to develop and maintain sufficient markets.

Correspondingly many other marketplace actions have historically represented large-scale efforts (for example, advertising), as it was generally believed that certain activities were particularly worthwhile because they produced significantly large returns. Today, technologies increasingly bridge these differences, providing firms of all sizes opportunities to engage in actions that have been previously limited to organizations with certain attributes (large numbers of employees, located in a number of cities, significant resources, and so forth). In the 1970s, for instance, a national mail out of advertising materials was generally limited to large firms who could afford the hardware and software capable of performing such large mail outs. Today, most modestly priced personal computers available in many small firms can easily handle such software requirements. As is evident from this example, new technologies have expanded opportunities for entrepreneurs, providing the ability to become more specialized with less regard for the size or economic strength of the firm. In a similar example, health care has benefited from the combination of technology and an entrepreneurial attitude. A number of nurses, for instance, have utilized technology to forge new businesses that focus on combining computer-based patient records and consulting (Simpson 1997). As the illustrations above note, the ability to manipulate data bases to collect very specific customer qualification data increases the ability of entrepreneurs to reach and service markets that were historically too large and costly for many small businesses and entrepreneurs. It is in this setting that new opportunities are opening.

New methods for managing data (Koreto 1996) and understanding markets (Pillsbury 1997) suggest opportunities for the technological entrepreneur are growing. For example, although Microsoft Windows software revolutionized the personal computer marketplace, the initial marketplace consideration of buyers was not the size of Microsoft, but instead the ability of their product (Windows) to enrich the productivity of users.

MANAGERIAL IMPACTS

Finding the Technological Entrepreneur

A shared primary quality (strong belief in own correctness) of the entrepreneur and technologist works as a deterrent in finding individuals who are able to coalesce both of these outlooks. Specifically because both of these individuals believe in their ability unfailingly to make the right decision at the right time (enter a new market, develop a new product, and so forth), the strength and conviction of such a viewpoint can interfere with the proper identification of these individuals. Furthermore, coupled with an insistence that their decisions and actions are always going to produce positive outcomes, assessing individuals for these qualities is a difficult task.

There are two primary sources (internal and external) of these types of employees. Initially and whenever possible, it makes sense to look for such an individual within your own organization. This approach is not only less expensive than the second method (external identification), it is also more expedient because these employees are usually physically more accessible. Additionally, contemporary information is available about their performance, work habits, on the job behaviors, and so forth under a variety of conditions. Critically, these individuals are likely to be only sparsely available within many organizations because the basis for hiring personnel is usually based on different criteria than finding workers with both technological and entrepreneurial traits.

Although some technological entrepreneurs may have risen through the employment nets, most are likely to be at the lower levels of organizations. This is because employees already possessing these qualities who have been employed at the firm for some time are likely to have become socialized through formal and informal organizational pressures, changing the basic mold of the individual away from the technological entrepreneur toward a traditional, single orientation employee framework.

When individuals are identified internally who have these qualities, they are likely going to need sufficient seasoning at different organizational levels and responsibilities before they can assume key responsibilities as a technological entrepreneur. As a result, converting or building employees with this outlook can be a timely activity that may take two to five years and a significant resource commitment to this individual. For example, it may be necessary to place this individual in several different organizational disciplines over a period of several years for the purpose of exposing him or her to a variety of working environments. Organizations selecting to cultivate the technological entrepreneur, therefore, must be willing to be patient as efforts are crafted to foster the individual. Care must also be taken under this approach not to place the individual(s) selected in an organizational setting where the desired qualities are diminished through an anti-socialization process. For example, if a developing technological entrepreneur is placed within a department where the manager sees little advantage in taking measured risks, the existence of such an attitude may diminish the employee's desire or interest in developing and applying this entrepreneurial skill.

In contrast, a quicker, although more risky approach, is the identification and hiring of these individuals externally. This approach is more risky primarily because of where these individuals are historically found, and the subsequent work socialization process to which they have likely been exposed in their career. Typically, the possession of both skills is necessary in smaller firms, where the combination of these attributes becomes a necessity of survival (in smaller organizations employees are often required to be more multifunctional than in larger companies). Thus, in a study of contrasts, entrepreneurial firms are usually innovative, flexible (Kraemer et al. 1996), and small (for example, Meeks and Linden 1994; Nikiforuk 1996), while larger companies face less risk (Ballantine, Cleveland, and Koeller 1993). In turn, these different environments create an atmosphere that may not always be conducive to the technological entrepreneur.

Although there are more technological entrepreneurs in smaller firms, their skills, demeanor, and interests may not be suited for placement within larger organizational structures (where bureaucracies are typically far more entangled). The primary danger in employing these individuals is generally the placement of a key employee within a structure in which they are not professionally suited or experienced. For example, in smaller firms, managerial decisions are more quickly made and the time to implement these decisions is comparatively small. In contrast, in larger firms, having managerial status does not necessarily transcend rapid actions, as key activities often require approval at a variety of different managerial levels. Accordingly, the difference in organizational bureaucracies can hinder the success or even willingness to work in this environment.

Furthermore, because technological entrepreneurs employed externally are more likely to be employed at a high organizational level, the danger in mistaken hiring has far greater implications. That is, when initially employed this individual typically comes into the firm with the organizational clout to make mistakes that are far reaching throughout the firm. Hence, because the employment of technological entrepreneurs from this sector can produce exceptional or terrible results, particular care has to be made in the employment of these individuals from this sector.

Integrating Activities

Successful firms are finding that simply having either an entrepreneurial outlook or a vision of technology is insufficient. Particularly evident among entrepreneurs who have discovered the need to combine operations and entrepreneurship (Brandt 1986; Morris and Trotter 1990; Pinchot 1985), the opportunity exists to integrate technology and an entrepreneurial vision. In this context, as entrepreneurial activities (Coviello 1996) and the influence of technology have grown in recent years, the returns for embracing a technological entrepreneurial spirit appear to be increasingly enticing. These returns are evident in a wide array of industries, such as forestry and wood (Baldwin 1997), publishing (Gremillion 1997), health care (Simpson 1997), and financial services (Goddard 1997), where the need exists to make strategic (Child 1972), purposeful (Van de Ven and Poole 1995), managerial decisions (Bartlett and Goshal 1996) that integrate technology with entrepreneurial opportunities. Impacted by factors such as the size of the firm (Fefer 1997) and the workers (for example, Stern 1996), not all organizations are candidates for this approach. Therefore, managers and organizations considering this roadway will have the most success if they carefully examine the totality of returns and pitfalls for embracing this decision.

6

The Influence of Technology on Marketing

Although technology over the next generation of users will influence every business function, there are few areas that will be impacted to the degree of the marketing organization. As external and internal operatives, the marketing department in most organizations is highly prone toward merging technologies and users. Accordingly, successful marketers will be those who are able to find strategic linkages with suppliers and customers via technology. Much like sharing other key resources, marketers who are able to commingle technologies, particularly information technologies, will share common paths that will tie the two parties into long-term relationships. For this reason, there are several critical issues that must be examined within the framework of how technology influences the roles of marketing.

In this context, the purpose of this chapter is to explore how technologies will directly impact the major functions of marketing (commonly thought of as product, pricing, promotion, and place or distribution). Addressing these major functions, however, is not the emphasis of this chapter. Instead, this chapter will explore what marketers can do to focus on emerging technologies within the context of taking advantage of their primary mission.

MARKETING MISSIONS

The basic mission of marketers in most organizations is to produce sufficient revenue to ensure that the organization is able to survive and grow. To accomplish this objective, marketers generally focus on four major areas of responsibility, which are also often referred to as the four P's. Each area represents a different scope of responsibility and job assignments, although no single area is considered more or less important than the others.

The first area is product and includes such decisions as product design, packaging, services with the products, and how they match up to existing or potential users. Although products and services may vary in their offerings, the product is one component of satisfying client needs.

The second area is pricing and addresses issues related to assigning proper marketplace value to a product and then ensuring this value is strategically implemented. Of course all products do not have the same value, and, therefore, marketers must determine what price the consumers are willing to pay considering the package of value they receive.

The third area is promotion, and it focuses on the communication and related processes that occur between the seller and existing or potential buyers. Done through a variety of integrated marketing communications (for example, advertising, personal selling, direct marketing, sales promotion, publicity, and public relations), the goal of communication is to coordinate all seller-initiated efforts to set up channels of information and persuasion to sell goods and services or promote an idea.

The fourth area is place or distribution. The emphasis in this dimension is on strategically moving products (even services) where customers can purchase them.

Intermixing throughout these dimensions, the marketer must develop the product, price it appropriately, promote it to customers, and then ensure that the product is available for buyers at the desired time and place. This integration of activities, therefore, becomes a critical element in understanding the role of technology and marketing. That is, the role of these functional areas to marketers is to place their strategic and operational efforts in closer proximity to buyers. It is this need to create closer customer proximity, therefore, that is the underlying purpose of this chapter.

STRATEGIC, ORGANIZATIONAL, AND MANAGERIAL IMPACTS OF TECHNOLOGY ON MARKETING FUNCTIONS

The impact of technology on marketers can be underscored by a primary overriding need of marketers. That is, to be successful, marketers must understand, predict, and react to customer needs. To do this requires linkages with customers and associated parties. Hence, based on the need for such attachments, there are selected areas that are dramatically impacted via technology that are within the framework of the marketing functions (product, place, promotion, and price). These areas are discussed in more detail next.

Communication

Marketing used to rely upon creative execution of promotional messages. However, today the creative aspect of the marketing program is based upon stronger and more detailed customer analysis (Nelson 1998). For instance, the Internet was once ignored by marketing departments. Today it is an integral part of most marketing strategies. Online advertising is booming. In the first half of 1998 online advertising spending in the United States totaled $774 million, double the year-earlier pace (Anders 1998). Online ad spending is not merely keeping pace with increased use of the Internet, it is rising appreciably faster. Marketers, such as Procter & Gamble, Unilever, and Gillette, who in the past spent as much as 80 percent of their ad budgets on television, realize the Internet is threatening to shatter the mass market into millions of individual consumers doing their own thing online. They recognize the importance of a new form of promotion, "word-of-mouse."

Some marketers wonder whether they can get enough response to justify the cost. Most advertisers pay at least as much to reach an Internet audience ($10 to $40 per 1,000 viewers) as they would for television or magazine ads. Creativity no longer dominates success. The most technologically sophisticated systems are necessary to take advantage of market opportunities. The successful application of technology to marketing problems will allow the development of more effective campaigns to build upon traditional marketing skills.

Because of the very nature of most business-related technologies, they typically in some manner enhance contact or communication between different parties. That is, business technologies generally improve the interaction between two or more parties, and in turn they provide some type of information to users. Accordingly, communication is often the first advantage cited as significantly improving through the usage of business technologies.

The basic question then becomes, what do improved communications mean directly to marketers? To answer this question, one must first examine the parties that engage in the exchange of information. To assess this flow of information, therefore, one must track information flows in a typical marketing or business organization, where most managers would be surprised by the dramatic dispersion of information that occurs through each decision, even those that are small, seemingly insignificant decisions. For instance, a marketing decision to improve compensation plans (for example, commission payments are changed) impacts many marketing (sales managers, sales people, marketing managers, compensation managers, contest administrators, and so forth) and non-marketing areas (for example, human resources, strategic planning, payroll, accounting). To modify a compensation plan successfully, it is often necessary to notify many parties of even small modifications in the marketing compensation packages.

However, despite the wide array of information dispersion, the question remains as to the underlying purpose or need for marketers to improve communications. Easily answered of course in an organization that adopts the marketing orientation (the entire firm is directed to the customer), the intended purpose of improving communications is directly or indirectly to enrich linkages between buyers and sellers. Although these linkages may be indirect (for example, better internal communication allows a firm to respond more rapidly to client needs), the foundation of improvements in communication has to be the enrichment of buyer-seller information (communication) flow. For example, as the improvement of communications occurs through technologies, the information available and internal or external information flows are improved. Hence, in such an environment, marketers are able to anticipate market needs more rapidly, as well as to respond to those needs.

Key to this issue is the transformation from mass marketing to database marketing. The purpose is not to acquire and store information for its own sake, but rather to drive individualized communications and generate sales. Marketing executives must use database technology to develop precise targets with matching promotional efforts. Gathering more information about customers to tailor messages will be important in differentiation strategies.

Accountability and Tracking Results

In one of the more interesting outcomes, the availability of technologies to marketers will have a dramatic impact on the tracking of results and the subsequent assessment of the productivity of individual stations, departments, districts and regions, and individuals. More specifically, the measurement of productivity has long been a critical issue in marketing organizations (Oliver and Anderson 1994) that has not been resolved except at the sales level. For instance, through tracking some common information, such as sales quotas, it is possible to determine the performance level of some sales professionals (for example, sales people, sales managers). However, in light of a shift from market share to relationship enrichment, the marketing department may focus more on service rather than selling (Scott 1998). We see that marketing no longer means sending a message out to the masses. It means incorporating a customer service attitude throughout the organization from production to logistics to customer service centers. Different performance measures will be required, and to be effective, this change should be thoroughly communicated to all levels of the corporation.

A most critical change, however, in the framework of introducing technology, can be seen in the context of tracking some types of information and subsequently assessing performance from this information. As business technologies are increasingly reaching the desk of each marketer, the ability to measure that individual's performance will increase. Consider, for example, the common utilization of personal computers by many field and staff marketers. Although the purpose of these computers has been to improve individual and group performance, the organization now has individualized tracking stations that are capable of recording a wide array of activities for each user (or a composite of users). Hence, as software is increasingly developed for unique applications, a component of this software will more frequently be demanded that will focus on tracking specific (and sometimes unusual) activities. For instance, as sales territories are constructed via the personal computer software by sales managers, the specific territory assignments and year-end results can later be used to determine if the sales manager responded to changes in business activities and individual performance outcomes of salespeople assigned to those territories.

Just as interesting, software can be designed that can track a variety of activities, not all of which are thought of as common. For example, improved tracking and assessment of productivity opportunities exist in personnel assignments, effective time management, resource allocations, budget decisions, and task accomplishments. Hallmark utilized cross-functional teams to develop a new lines of cards. By utilizing technology and bringing various groups together, the new line was introduced to the market eight months ahead of the normal schedule.

Rapid Response and Client Feedback

Being able to respond quickly is an obvious advantage in some situations, and often is a requirement for other marketers. Given that the emphasis of marketers is the customer, part of this process is being able to assess the ongoing needs of clients, and in turn respond rapidly to certain situations. Consider, for example, when customers become dissatisfied over the condition of a purchase. If the marketer is aware of this situation, he or she can identify the evolving problem and resolve it as rapidly as possible. Thus, initially the ability of technology to exchange information rapidly with others often allows marketers to anticipate situations through changing conditions and respond to those situations.

Through information technologies, marketers can design systems (especially with client approval) that allow for the direct connection between the client and the marketer. For instance, through information technologies clients and sellers can be linked electronically to provide the seller feedback on the performance of the product or other, affiliated information. Accordingly, technological connections between clients and sellers work best when the buyer actively encourages such connections. Under such a system, marketers are able to compile information that suggests a problem might exist before it becomes a problem. For instance, if marketers are remotely notified of rapid changes in inventory of a retail outlet through the direct connection between checkout, available inventories, and the seller, new products can be rushed to the client before a pending problem becomes critical. Hence, connecting customers and sellers provides a basis for identifying problems and subsequently responding to them as well.

In addition to rapid response, business technologies provide a more important, overriding quality: feedback. Sellers constantly note that buyers provide too little information too late. Coupled with the opportunity to provide information that is frequently provided in a format that is not consistent with what the seller needs, information is often distorted between what the buyer needs and what the seller provides. As a result and through the proper usage of information technologies, buyers and sellers can create formal mechanisms to ensure that usable, appropriate information is available to buyers.

Partnering

The creation of technological linkages between buyers and sellers will create new types of partnerships that to date have only been discussed or existed in selected situations. That is, the opportunity to share information electronically increases occasions when data that are highly confidential will be shared with another business. General Electric, for example, uses cross-company teams with its customer, Southern California Electric. They reduced outage time and costs (caused by turbine shutdowns) by 50 percent through the usage of enhanced technology.

Under such an environment, customers will have to determine the degree to which they are willing to share such private information. Correspondingly, marketers will have to make significant commitments or determine the degree to which they are willing to commit to having access to such confidential information. Properly balanced, technology provides opportunities for new partnerships with strong internal links to be formed. Misused, such linkages become the ropes of mistrust, from which seller and buyer reputations may be damaged or destroyed.

Forecasting

The rapid collection of information provides a basis to anticipate where future needs and subsequent marketing decisions, activities, and strategies must be directed. For instance, through the complete and rapid tracking of delivery schedules, it is possible to assess very accurately the impact of three inches of snow on the delivery of products via several different delivery routes. Hence, when properly structured, the nature of information technologies can be used to enhance critical forecasting needs.

By their very nature, information technologies provide raw data that are often usable or easily convertible to proper formatting for more traditional computer input. It is the accessibility of information through information technologies from customers that often provides an initial basis for empirical forecasting. Marketers who have access to critical information (for example, customer trends, competitive advertising strategies) are well positioned to take advantage of empirical forecasting that engenders competitive advantages in many marketplace situations.

Marketers who are able to develop close partnerships with customers are those who will be able to utilize first the integration of technologies to blend with customer needs through an effective forecasting system. Of course for such a system to work, the customer must clearly see the benefits when marketers are able to forecast customer needs. For example, if the seller is able to anticipate that a buyer will need new inventories at a particular time, the utilization of just-in-time inventories to satisfy the needs of the buyer provides significant financial advantages for the customer. In this example, the ability to purchase products only moments before they are resold provides a solid benefit that can be seen in the context of economic gain to the buyer.

Correspondingly, in cases where close partnerships do not exist and the ability to acquire information from clients does exist via technology, forecasting from these data also provides rich benefits. In such cases, marketers will be able to utilize such information to forecast customer needs, from which trust, commitment, and strong relational ties can be built with sellers. This of course is more difficult, but it does provide an objective for marketers who are attempting to integrate into the culture of the buyer.

Marketers, therefore, seeking this benefit must look for methods to blend the technologies of the client and themselves. The greater the commingling, the more enhanced opportunities exist for utilizing information technologies to gain competitive advantages.

7

Managing Employees: New Challenges and Opportunities through Technology

The nature of technology has dramatically changed the contemporary work environment (for example, Fleming 1997). Although some of these changes are obvious (for example, communication of critical information, storage of long-term customer buying habits, empirically forecasting buying trends), other modifications that have occurred within the organization as the result of technology are just as important but often less visible. For example, although computers have changed many of the recordkeeping processes used to record sales, marketing organizations have had to dedicate resources to training salespeople and sales managers how to use these computers. Accordingly, although the scope of these changes occurs within a wide spectrum, few are as likely to be critical to the firm as the impact that technology has on the work force. Yet, few discussions are available that actually discuss this evolution that is increasingly impacting the business domain.

Within this evolving environment of information technologies, this chapter will focus on how contemporary work forces can be effectively introduced to and integrated with these potential conflicts and opportunities through technologies. For example, the evolution of desk top conferencing will allow the expansion of managerial control. In turn, the growth of responsibilities offers a number of opportunities and challenges that technologically oriented organizations must address, although many of these conditions have not yet been considered in terms of their impacts. In this context, this chapter will discuss how the integration of technologies will require different organizational socialization and management (for example, employment) practices.

TECHNOLOGY CHALLENGES AND OPPORTUNITIES

Driven by technology, changes have and will continue to occur in a host of areas, including employee responsibilities, capabilities, interests, subordinate-employee interactions, and internal and external communications. For example, because information technologies increase the availability of knowledge to the work force, managers will increasingly become more informed about a wider range of discipline and functional information. As an illustration of this evolution, marketers will become more aware of costing practices that in their estimation might unnecessarily increase the costs of products (which in turn might increase their prices, making them more difficult to sell). Correspondingly, accountants may discover that marketers are selling products at prices they consider below real costs. As a result, opportunities are created through technology (for example, computerization) to foster significant cross-functional knowledge that can be helpful in avoiding these mistakes.

In a setting where information is more readily available, corporations will be afforded opportunities to develop managers with broader, more extensive cross-functional knowledge and skills. Viewed in another context, managers will develop knowledge and understanding about areas outside of their traditional, educational, and work experience expertise. The growth of information technologies (computers, Internet, teleconferencing, and so forth) has provided more opportunities for employees to have access to a wider frame of information than has ever existed in the history of commerce. For example, the Internet provides a basis to begin searching for additional knowledge about competitive products that can be used to gain a differential advantage. Salespeople can use the Internet to assess existing competitive pricing, advertising, and even the delivery schedule of competitive products. Viewed as a proactive perspective, firms desiring to expand the knowledge of the work force through information technologies will find a great number of opportunities.

Although initially this perspective offers some significant advantages (for example, better decisions), this approach also encourages the development of other problems, as managers develop the ability to expand existing knowledge into functional areas that are outside their expertise (for example, marketers gaining engineering knowledge). Thus, saying that "a little knowledge is a dangerous thing" provides an accurate barometer of this condition. That is, although it is evident that an employee may be lacking in information, he or she may also have too much information, as the growth of technologies allows employees to seek information that may well be beyond the scope of responsibilities of traditional employees.

Because the expansion of knowledge can be obtained from many avenues (for example, Internet, internal computing functions), it becomes difficult to limit actual access once it has been provided. Consider computer hackers who penetrate internal company computer systems. Although gaining such access can be accomplished, the necessary computerization of records, processes, strategies, prices, resources, and so forth simply expands opportunities for employees to overindulge in this area. Hence, the growth of technologies allows employees to broaden their frame of knowledge far beyond existing levels to the point where the additional knowledge may be disruptive to the organization. Expanding on the previous illustration, marketers can use computer data bases to examine more closely costing strategies utilized by the internal accounting department. Then through an external search, the marketers may discover or broaden their knowledge about the pricing strategies utilized by competitors, as well as information about common costing approaches, accounting practices in this industry, and so forth. Armed with this information, the marketer may soon conclude that he or she is in a position to assess and propose costing strategies used by his/ or her accounting department. Not surprisingly, technological inequilibrium may result in internal organizational strife and conflict. In turn, organizations are faced with the challenge of redeveloping new levels of employee technological equilibrium.

Technological equilibrium is a state where information technologies have provided knowledge to the employee designed to broaden his or her expertise. Technological equilibrium occurs when the individual is provided just enough knowledge via information technologies. This balance is known as technological equilibrium.

STRATEGIC IMPACTS

The strategic implications of understanding the impact of technologies on employees rests on the long-term implications that are critical. Examples of these implications are identified in Table 7.1.

As Table 7.1 illustrates, there are a host of long-term strategic issues related to the use of technology that must be considered when adopting technology. Critical to this process, however, is for the adopting

TABLE 7.1
Long-term Implications of Merging Technologies and Employees

Interfacing
Training and development (remaining current)
Hiring of employees (identification, selection, and so forth)
Identification of early technological adopters and key reference group leaders
Resource commitment
Top management commitment
Job capabilities are updated
Evolving the entire work force, not selected key employees

---

organization to view the adoption and utilization of technologies as a long-term project within the context of a long-term organizational vision. That is, for the adoption of technologies to be successful, their socialization into the work force must take place and be seen as an ongoing project.

If, however, the organizational processes are designed to enjoin employees with technology on a one-time basis (for example, a single training program), over time the problems of this strategy will be obvious (for example, turnover, lost skills, outdated technologies).

The following subsections address in additional detail the issues identified in Table 7.1.

Interfacing

One of the most interesting and perhaps least understood long-term implications of merging employees and technologies is the change in human interfacing that is occurring as the result of information technologies. Put in another context, few managers recognize that technology will change the basic premise of how the interaction between employees and subordinates occurs.

In the 1970s, most interactions within the work force occurred via face-to-face contact. For example, peers in accounting and sales often meet to discuss tracking sales and profits. Supplemented with telephone and mail service, most contact between employees has historically hinged on some personal contact (voice inflection, facial expressions, and so forth) between the parties, fostering an environment where personal communication is a critical element in successful interchanges.

With the rapid growth in information technologies, however, these business exchanges have become increasingly less personalized. For instance, the widespread use of e-mail has greatly reduced personal meetings and telephone contact. As a result, the nature of business relationships has changed dramatically. Consider in this context the rapid growth of chat rooms over the Internet. In these rooms, individuals discuss a variety of issues, some of which are quite personal. For instance, although some chat rooms are dedicated to sports, politics, and entertainment, others are directed to those who desire to create and maintain personal relationships. Often carried out without having actual personal contact (no meetings or phone calls), these relationships have redefined the concept of what composes, and the criteria for, an individual relationship.

Similarly, we can expect to see the same happening within business encounters. That is, individuals will increasingly rely less on personal contact within business relationships. Although what this will mean is not totally certain at this time, it does bring into question what the impact will be on issues such as trust, compassion, believability, commitment, and understanding within the context of personal relationships. How will these and other personal qualities that have been important for so long in business relationships be reshaped through the growth of information technologies? In this vein, what will define professional relationships, and how will they evolve, maintain, and dissolve? Although such answers are not clear, it is evident that because technologies are reshaping the nature of business relationships, successful business organizations will seek the answers to these questions.

Training and Development

Unfortunately for many organizations, training employees in current technologies is a wasted effort. As significant resources are placed in initially updating employees on technologies, these efforts often represent a lavish expenditure designed to satisfy short-term needs. More importantly, little effort is often placed in ensuring that employees remain current over the long term, creating an environment where technology is updated but the users are not. Yet, for some organizations an opportunity is created when competitors fail to engage in long-term programs. By making the commitment to remain technologically current, competitive firms are able to address the changing environment. As such, training by itself is often seen by these firms as not a particularly difficult task. Utilized as a short-term process, they understand that it is fairly simple to train employees initially on contemporary technologies.

In contrast, however, competitive firms have a tendency to ensure that their employees are included in a long-term development process. This requires a commitment that entails the forecasting and training of employees in emerging technologies over their employment lifetime. It is our estimation that because this is far more difficult than training employees, it is seldom accomplished in many organizations.

Hiring

A primary strategic issue that has to be considered is the hiring of employees. Hiring processes must be aligned to ensure that new employees are consistent in their interests in integrating technologies within the scope of their job responsibilities. Not limited to certain employees, the strategic assumption has to rest on the belief that every job responsibility and every employee at some time will be expected to integrate technologies within their positional responsibilities. For some positions the time for making this decision is obviously at the time of employment. For other positions the time may be later. For instance, maintenance workers and accountants both have to be included within this framework. Although the accountants may be expected to utilize information technologies immediately, the maintenance worker may at some future time also be expected to record work activities (for example, equipment utilized) on a computer. Hence, although both may work with information technologies, their work level and expertise required would vary.

This approach does not suggest that all employees must have the same level of technological familiarity, comfort, or skill level. Instead, this strategic vision simply recognizes that each position has a level of acceptable skill and interest, and for successful strategic hiring purposes this level must be determined for each specific position. Hence, human esources or other employment functions must assume the responsibility of both prevailing and future technological expectations for each position. For example, if accountants are expected to be able to program in an evolving language, hiring practices must reflect this need. Obviously accomplished through open dialogue with functional managers, assessing these needs is not an easy task.

Particularly difficult, however, will be forecasting the technological needs of typically non-technical employees. As previously noted, areas such as maintenance are particularly difficult to forecast, as little has historically been expected of many of these types of job functions.

New hiring practices will also have to be considered. For instance, some temporary workers have fared well in today's fast-changing, high tech world. Some business system analysts move from one job to another taking their computer skills with them and mastering new skills in the process (Schellhardt 1999). Becoming a jack-of-all-trades allows these workers to stay atop of their field and make more money. This type of hiring practice needs to be viewed in comparison to providing training internally to employees.

After a level of expectation is determined, however, assessment measures must be constructed to determine the level of the prospective employee. Thus, determinations must be made with respect to what an employee can and will do technologically. This of course can be accomplished via a number of different techniques, such as technological audits and interviews.

Identification of Early Technological Adopters and Key Reference Group Leaders

Marketers have long understood that all individuals do not accept products at the same rate. For instance, the first users of computers were a small minority of individuals, as most people avoided for a variety of reasons the intervention of computer technology into their home and office. In another context, some people enjoy the risk of trying products before others, taking pleasure in trying new ventures, products, and so forth. In contrast, however, there are other individuals who prefer to wait before trying new products. For instance, not every consumer who had a personal computer and who could afford and had a need for a color printer purchased one initially. Some people are willing to wait exceptionally long periods of time before making a purchase of a product despite its appearance of matching their needs. They make this decision of inactivity based on several possible criteria, such as the belief that waiting reduces the risk of failure associated with new products. Accordingly, understanding the process of adoption provides business organizations a critical road map to introducing and improving the level of technology acceptance throughout the firm. By accepting, in effect, that not all employees will accept new technologies at the same level of intensity over the same period, this provides strategic information with respect to technological integration.

To introduce and integrate new technologies it is important to identify two major groups of employees. The first group is innovators: those individuals who are willing to try new ideas, products, and applications. These individuals are venturesome and are more willing to take risks — a requirement of innovation. That is, the first people to adopt a new technology incur the risk that the product will not work as well as expected and possibly that they will be embarrassed by a bad decision. Consider, for example, the risk of those of us (both authors included) who bought a Sony Betamax video cassette recorder in the 1980s. Not many people were willing to be the first to invest $1,200 for the equipment or to pay $79.95 for videos that were soon replaced by the VHS format.

These innovators tend to be younger, higher in social status, and better educated than later adopter groups. They interact mostly with other innovators and rely heavily on impersonal informational sources, rather than other people, to satisfy their information needs. They usually have a broader range of interests than non-innovators.

Through the identification of these employees, management is able strategically to place new technologies with individuals willing to make new applications with minimal pre-constructed resistances and bias. Ideally, these individuals will provide a barometer as to the abilities of the new technologies to be functionally acceptable within the immediate organization. Later, these individuals provide a bridge into the acceptance of technologies by other groups.

The second group of employees crucial in introducing new technology is the group who are somewhat reluctant to adopt new products, ideas, and so forth but who have peer respect and who are typically seen by others in the work force as leaders. Other employees frequently look up to these individuals, as they have gained a great deal of intraorganizational respect (as a result of work performance, abilities, outlook, leadership, intelligence, social standing, and so forth). By identifying these leaders, management can achieve technology osmosis throughout the organization. Based on the idea that other employees will note the satisfaction, success, accomplishments, and so forth that these key influence centers experience with technology, other employees will more aggressively seek to follow these individuals into the technological domain.

MANAGERIAL IMPACTS

Technologies are believed to impact the work environment. Interestingly, however, particularly given the significant investment required of technology, direct evidence linking technology and employee and firm productivity is lacking. Thus, in an environment where there is wide acceptance and strong beliefs that technology has a positive impact on output, this is chiefly an unproven phenomenon (Delone and McLean 1992). Correspondingly, related managerial issues with respect to the impact of technology directly on the work force remain basically unaddressed.

Even with the very few explorations that have investigated the direct impact of technology on productivity, the direct influence remains difficult to assess from both an empirical and conceptual basis. However, logic tells us that the implementation of correctly installed and managed technology is a useful and strategically beneficial process. Within this framework, the charge of management is to introduce appropriate technologies responsibly within the firm. Occurring in an environment where failing to remain technologically current seems to guarantee increased opportunities for failure, management must balance the needs of the marketplace with the needs and abilities of the firm.

For management, therefore, it is often necessary to spend a great deal of resources on technology, often with no evidence that directly links technology and performance. Consider whether management would engage in other expenditures under similar conditions. Would management for instance approve opening a new sales office without indications that such a commitment would lead to specific dollar returns? Not likely, as such investments are typically expected to create specific returns. Accordingly the magnitude of these returns plays a critical role in determining if these actions are actually implemented. Thus, management expects and would forecast a return based on such factors as the marketplace, competition, new products being introduced, and the ability of the sales office to generate more revenue than the costs required.

Yet in the contemporary technology-driven environment, assessing the level of expenditures that management must make to ensure that the technology and the employees are aligned is difficult if not impossible. For example, can the financial returns to a firm on a new computer system be accurately determined? In creating a very difficult investment-return situation, such calculations are not possible in many if not most cases. To maximize returns on technology, management must ensure that the employees are positioned to benefit from the technology, although the measurement of the actual benefits may not be clear or precise. In turn, the ability to reach this status cultivates a term we shall refer to as technological alignment.

ORGANIZATIONAL IMPACTS

Technological Alignment

Technological alignment is a state that refers to a balance of four components: understanding the organizational employees (abilities, skills, needs, and so forth), the conditions of the job (for example, technical support, activities the employee must accomplish), the willingness of top management to bring these elements together, and the merging of technologies within the internal work force.

Several key premises are underscored by technological alignment. One such premise is that not all firms, situations, markets, and so forth are good choices for internally introducing technology. Management must accept that the introduction of technology is not enough within the firm to ensure its organizational socialization. For instance, placing personal computers on the desks of many top executives in the early 1980s was not enough to ensure that they would use these tools. More recently we can see that many managers have equally avoided the use of e-mail.

In this state of technological alignment, there are several possible conditions. During the state of being under technologically aligned, the firm does not have the correct conditions to install and maintain new technologies. Installation is just part of this process, as maintenance is at least if not more important over the long term. When faced with this condition, management must first make sufficient changes to ensure that technologies can be successfully deployed. For example, if the current employees lack adequate understanding and training in the operation of their personal computers, it would be extremely difficult for their employees to use e-mail among fellow workers. Although generalizations are always difficult to make, it does appear that for the most part, companies that have conducted business the same way for many years (for example, small family-owned businesses) have a greater tendency to allow themselves to become technologically under aligned.

In contrast, over alignment occurs when a firm has an excess of technological conditions (for example, large number of employees knowledgeable in the specifics of the technology). Interestingly, this condition also presents certain concerns to the firm. The risk of this condition to the organization is that because the environment is rich with opportunities to use technologies as well as individuals who desire to try out these technologies, attempts will be made to place technologies in situations that are not strategically sound for the firm. For instance, this condition often can be seen when an employee decides to insert a new expert system that has not been thoroughly tested and has not yet been assessed by the proper internal organizational experts (technical, software, subject matter, and so forth). Under these conditions, the placement of such a system could obviously lead to a number of significant problems. Our observation indicates more technically oriented positions (for example, engineers) and companies (for example, telecommunications) have a greater tendency to become over aligned because of their basic nature and mission to seek out and utilize advancing technologies, coupled with their employees, who in general have a higher degree of technological knowledge and interest than many others.

In the middle of under and over alignment, rests proper technological alignment, and as this term suggests, the positioning within the firm cannot be improved. This state is more likely a vision than an actual condition. That is, firms should seek this status but not be surprised when they fail to achieve it. Proper alignment, of course, indicates that the conditions are right (employees, management support, the environment, and so forth) for the deployment and ongoing continuation of technologies.

Determining Alignment

From these and other examples, we can see that the introduction of technology within the organization must be accompanied by the appropriate usage of the technologies. Because of the existence of certain deficiencies that exist within all firms (for example, money, skilled employees), there are occasions when organizations should not introduce or even consider upgrading technology internally. Consider the significant number of staff hours required to introduce any change, much less one that is as different as a new technology. For example, if there is no real time available for employees to dedicate to learning a new technology (for example, accountants during tax season), investments in this area may not be sound.

Correspondingly, there are other firms that are better positioned to introduce and socialize technologies. Based on a variety of reasons (for example, they have the resources to successfully introduce technologies, technical staff to support such introductions), the alignment of the internal structure and conditions of the firm works to their advantage in implementing new technologies.

Of a more perplexing and typically quite common situation, however, are those firms that are unsure of their status. That is, no clear path or message suggests that the introduction of technology or the withholding of technology is the correct strategy. This middle ground is a far more difficult and common situation, as it places a great deal of strain on the ability of top management to identify the actual degree to which they are aligned, the ability to make adjustments, and the timing of the technological adoption. For this reason, we offer Table 7.2, which identifies several key questions that help with the identification of the degree to which a firm is capable of being technologically aligned.

TABLE 7.2
Assessing Technological Alignment

Is training required and provided?
Will the use of technologies be reinforced?
Does sufficient technical support exist?
Is top management committed to introducing new technologies?
Will top, middle, and lower management use the technologies?
Is the firm structured to allow the use of the technologies?
What are the negative and positive implications of the technology?
Is the technology consistent with the abilities of employees?
Will this technology enhance or maintain competitive positioning?

As identified in Table 7.2, there are a number of questions and answers that may lead to an assessment of the degree to which a firm is technologically aligned. Important to this process, however, management should do this assessment on a systematic basis. The need to do such an assessment systematically is based on understanding that because of competitive pressures and the strong motive of profit, technologies often flow throughout the business environment rapidly. In such a dynamic environment there is a need for those firms seeking to be aligned to constantly assess and reassess their status, making changes within the firm as needed. In contrast, however, firms that choose to utilize this audit irregularly should therefore not be surprised when their alignment does not meet the desired goal. In the cases of firms that hire employees on an irregular schedule, making alignment adjustments could take years. Thus, a systematic audit of the status of their technological alignment is critical for firms to remain strategically current.

8

Technological Synergy:
The Organizational Integration of
Information Systems

At the center of business technologies over the next decade, within the context of both contemporary uses and evolving demands, will be the information systems department and its personnel. The information systems department is where information technology changes originate within most business organizations and where they occur most frequently. Specifically, the core of these changes is often driven by technologies that are based in, controlled by, or used in innovations or applied within basic information systems functions. For example, emerging software applications are the basis for the management and control of many technologies that will be utilized outside the core of the information systems mission. A critical point is that although the information systems personnel may assume responsibilities for the ongoing maintenance of the equipment, the use of technology will be primarily external to the information systems department.

As a result of the coalescing of technologies into more centralized management circles, the information systems department is and will remain at the forefront of a vast number of technology-related changes that are likely to occur within business organizations during the next decade. Specifically because these technological changes are so closely linked to information systems, it is critical to examine the impacts of technology within the field of information systems. That is, to ensure the successful development and implementation of technologies within the firm, what can the

information systems group do to enhance this process? It is within this
vein that this chapter will examine from a managerial perspective the
scope and impact of these evolutions within the firm and explore the
impacts to the information systems department that will occur as a result
of this reshifting of what we refer to as technological synergy outside the
traditional information systems scope of responsibility. Corresponding to
this synergy, this section will explore the underlying roles of information
systems personnel in light of their changing relationships with professionals in other departments. As part of this process, this discussion will
also include an examination of the process by which the information systems department will converge with other departmental functions and
consequently the options that this approach provides management.

STRATEGIC IMPACTS

Technological synergy is a process of blending different functions and
personnel through technology. More specifically, technological synergy
occurs when a variety of different positions, departments, and responsibilities are brought together in an organizational merging through technology for the purpose of enriching the total output of all the parties. For
example, through the training of sales personnel in the use of computers,
coupled with the increased availability of computerization to sales organizations, sales managers are better able to track such critical elements as
buying trends of customers, selling inroads made by competitors, and
changes in prices of new products. As a result, the sales manager is
increasingly able to construct a local strategy that takes advantage of this
knowledge, which reduces the need for national or external intervention
by other corporate marketing personnel (national sales manager, manager
of strategic planning, and so forth). In turn, the sales manager is afforded
a host of additional advantages, many of which did not exist prior to having such information computerized.

Before we continue beyond this point, however, we should point out
that there is also a contrast to this perspective. That is, although such
merging occurs on a systematic basis in many firms, this process does not
automatically enrich the output of the organization. That is, the bringing
together of resources through technology does not automatically engender
organizational benefits. In fact, for this process to be of particular profit
for the firm, this process must be seen and implemented strategically.

Hence, the positive premise of technology synergy is that it enriches
the capabilities and performance of through the aggressive, strategic utilization of technology. In effect, this process expands the abilities of users

TABLE 8.1
Advantages of Technological Synergy

Expands the abilities of users
Technological needs can be better forecast
Increases interorganizational communication
New technologies can be more easily implemented
Increases availability of information within the firm
Shapes employees to be more sensitive to organizational needs
Increases the productivity of the individual and organization
Interflow of information provides cross training of personnel
Allows installed technologies to be more specific to user needs

---

through the enlargement of those areas that they can accomplish. In this vein, advantages of technological synergy are detailed more specifically in Table 8.1.

As noted in Table 8.1, many advantages are provided to organizations that make the conscious decision to engage in technological synergy. For example, through the strategic use of technological synergy, the organization is able to expand the abilities of local departmental (non-information systems) personnel by assigning information systems personnel to work with other employees who are external to the information systems department. This can be illustrated by the salesperson that has been schooled by an information systems professional in the correct utilization of expert systems to implement local selling strategies. If the salesperson is able to utilize such a system successfully to construct an acceptable (for example, preapproved by the marketing department) pricing contract for the customer, this expands the abilities of the salesperson to work in an extended area of expertise (for example, pricing). Thus, when this salesperson is promoted or transferred to the marketing department, he or she is better prepared to deal with these issues. Correspondingly, because a basic premise of technology is to enrich the performance of the user, this often includes expanding his or her area of expertise.

In turn, such expansions often include developing additional knowledge, skills, expertise, and so forth that are outside the historical responsibilities of the individual. Hence, such expansions broaden the basic abilities of the employee. In this vein, it is expected that as technologies increasingly become available to consumers at an early age and the socialization processes and restraints to learning technologies decrease, the formal lines of organizational authority and responsibility in some firms will become more blurred and less precise. In fact, we anticipate that in some organizations, employees will be required to become minimally cross-trained in several functional areas of responsibility (for example, accounting and sales) because of the availability of information through technologies.

Corresponding to this initial advantage, through the integration of information systems professionals throughout the organization (that is, technological synergy), companies are better qualified to anticipate and forecast contemporary and future technological needs. Consider the critical nature of this advantage, whereas changes that often occur in competitive market situations are often noted by competitors after a loss (for example, market share) has occurred. For this reason, understanding, anticipating, and being able to implement new technologies offer businesses a significant advantage that translates to real value. This advantage can be illustrated when the finance department of a large corporation has been introduced to new conferencing equipment and techniques that reduce time, travel, and money expenditures of departmental members meeting with field personnel. Specifically, through the usage of sophisticated technologies, corporate and field personnel can meet via such mechanisms as interactive television.

Through the assignment of an information systems professional to work with finance department members on this venture, several benefits are incurred by the organization. First, by working with an internal professional (for example, finance department employee), this individual can assess the degree to which the intricacies of the technologies are effectively being utilized. That is, is the finance department getting maximum value and usage out of the conferencing system? As a result, when total effectiveness of this or another technology is not reached, the information systems professional can offer meaningful suggestions for improvement. Importantly, however, these suggestions will be constructed based on the practical abilities of the technology, as well as an understanding of that particular firm's willingness and abilities to engage in such efforts, expenditures, and so forth (for example, the information systems employee knows if such suggestions can practically be implemented internally).

Correspondingly, the information systems professional can work closely with the finance contact person and can accurately forecast the evolving needs of the functional department. Importantly, experience has demonstrated that although information systems and functional professionals (for example, finance department member) can somewhat forecast the technological needs of a department, the most effective method of this occurs through teaming both parties to provide mutual benefits. This seems to be most effective when the information systems professional is assigned to the functional department.

Another advantage noted in Table 8.1 is that the implementation of technologies is more easily accomplished through technological synergy. Consider the situation where the information systems professional is working closely with the auditing manager. As more advanced technologies are developed and readied for organizational implementation, the information systems professional is able to overcome personal and professional resistance to the acceptance of these technologies through his or her personal understanding and knowledge of the individual(s) in auditing. That is, a previously developed professional relationship allows the information systems employee to work within the confines of the personality, motivation, and so forth of that functional person, using this information to implement new technologies. As an illustration, if the information systems professional has noted that a particular manager is insecure about his or her understanding of a new technology, an increased emphasis can be given in that functional area to the training of auditing personnel in technology implementation. As a result of such an approach, fewer roadblocks to the implementation of new technologies are likely to exist, as developing and understanding personal relationships allow for a more intimate view of the individual(s) who will be key in implementing new advances. Coupled with the historical trend of consumers in general to resist the new insertion of technologies into their lives, this effort can become critical in many organizations. Thus, before this particular benefit is considered as part of technological syngery, management must examine the targeted personnel and their attitudes to determine the degree to which the receiving individual(s) is receptive to new technologies.

A critical benefit to technological synergy rests in the opportunity that this process allows technologies to be shaped according to the needs of users. Consider, for example, the large amount of software that has proliferated throughout many organizations with little regard to the explicit needs of specific users. As a result, users are often left with the task of trying to determine to what degree and how software can be shaped for that particular user. Of course, some users are more easily able to engage in such engineering and application construction. In contrast, however, a vast number of other users are less capable of making such individualistic applications, which in turn often results in software that could be useful being left unused. For this reason, many early creators of quality spreadsheets had difficulty in selling their software. In turn, those firms that made spreadsheets easy to shape around the specific needs of users experienced far greater sales opportunities and marketplace penetration. For this reason, we propose that technological synergy is a critical task, which, when properly done, provides significant benefits.

These benefits of technological synergy, however, come with some costs. That is, to be successful in this venture, the organization must be overtly willing to invest in this activity, seeing the integration of information systems personnel and activities as a worthwhile venture. Accordingly, the following section addresses the importance of understanding that utilization of technological synergy may result in some problems.

THE COST OF TECHNOLOGICAL SYNERGY

Because enlarging or redirecting organizational resources requires an enlargement of traditional capabilities and the historical emphasis on information systems personnel, the organizational price of such an approach must be carefully considered. That is, shifting information systems personnel and their historical responsibilities within an organization can foster some unexpected negative dividends.

A specific example that illustrates the type of problems fostered through technological synergy can be seen in the conflicts that will arise among employees. For instance, expanding the traditional skills of employees through technology is almost guaranteed to create some confusion and even jealously among certain organizational members. As an illustration of this, consider the situation where the abilities of the sales manager are expanded due to his or her work with computer technology (for example, expert systems) in constructing local advertising strategies.

Initially, to utilize an expert system to construct a local adverting strategy, the sales manager will need to be trained in that specific expert system. Likely this would require the efforts of a variety of organizational personnel (for example, an information systems professional, an advertising manager, and a marketing manager). Once this training has been accomplished, however, the sales manager will independently be making critical decisions that have historically been made by other personnel (for example, a regional advertising manager). As the sales manager expands his or her scope of responsibility and expertise in making these decisions, it is very probable some of the responsibilities of the individuals formerly assigned this task (for example, the advertising manager) will simultaneously decrease. In turn, it would not be unusual for the individual being replaced to become unhappy with the decreased responsibilities. For this reason, some employees may be content to see this process fail.

The point of this illustration is, of course, to note that when significant changes are made within the organizational ranks, these changes have to be viewed in a broad context. That is, questions must be asked and answered as to the total impact of these modifications within the framework of both the potential positive and negative outcomes. For this reason, we stress that although technological synergy offers a number of positive benefits and for many firms it represents a critical organizational activity, its implementation increases opportunities and occasions in which the flow of technology throughout the firm will not be successful. Hence, the cost of technological synergy is such that some organizations may not find it a rewarded effort.

ORGANIZATIONAL IMPACTS

Underscoring the basis of technological synergy is that such offerings are provided through an expansion of the services some personnel provide. That is, the premise of this concept rests on the ability of individuals within the firm to integrate technology services. As a result, critical to the success of this venture is the willingness of technical support personnel to work with more traditionally non-technical personnel (for example, maintenance) for the sole purpose of using technology to enhance the output of these less technical personnel and their functional departments. Correspondingly, the non-technical personnel must be willing to allow these technical personnel to invade their work space sharing ideas and concerns for the designed purpose to improve their output through enhanced technical productivity. Therefore, as with most key activities, the success of the process rests on the ability and willingness of the employees to allow this process to take place. If in fact employees decide that technological synergy is not in their best interest, it will not be successful.

To ensure the success of this process, therefore, management should seek to offer positive inducements for the process to occur. Critical for these offerings to take place, however, is that management must either have a sense of the true value of implementing the technology (which is extremely difficult to do), or management must be willing to make assumptions about the long-term worth of the technology. Once a value is assigned to the technology, management can subsequently make meaningful incentives to employees who successfully engage in this process (for example, cash or prize rewards, contests). If specific value cannot be assigned to this implementation process, then assessments of efforts to use technological synergy must be included as part of the annual employee performance evaluation. For instance, the sales manager discussed earlier is rewarded for the successful utilization of the expert system as part of a locally implemented advertising program.

Typically total integration cannot and should not be left to traditional intraorganizational communication processes (for example, meetings, memos). Instead, for the process of integration to be successful, it is essential for the firm to place information systems personnel who are familiar with and understand the applications of the intended technology throughout the firm. This is a critical endeavor because the acceptance or rejection of any new technology is more dependent upon the attitudes, beliefs, and perceptions of the users of the technology than it is contingent upon the immediate advantages that the technology provides. For example, if a new software program allows sales managers to assess and assign local sales territories more effectively, this program will only be useful if the sales managers actually utilize and incorporate it throughout their sales force. If the program is not utilized the benefits or advantages it brings the sales force are meaningless. This process can be further illustrated through an information systems employee who is assigned to work with auditors (who are external to the information systems group). In this example, the information systems employee must work with the auditor, ensuring that he or she is maximizing the ability of the existing computer system to accomplish the tasks desired (for example, track, record, and analyze appropriate data).

As is illustrated in both of these examples, technological synergy is only effective when both parties (for example, the information systems professional and auditor or sales professional) openly engage in clear communication with the other party. Correspondingly, a single employee can hinder or even terminate the movement of technology throughout the firm.

Although there are a number of methods that can be utilized to enrich integration, the most critical component is how the information systems department views its counterparts in other functional areas. We are not suggesting that information systems personnel be disseminated organizationally in a form of technological banishment, to other departments. Instead, we are proposing that successful synergy will exist when the information systems department and associated personnel understand the information systems group is in essence a service function. Hence, the responsibility of the information systems personnel is to serve other departments and assist their personnel in accomplishing their objectives. As such, the basic mission of the information systems department is to engage in a form of internal buyer-seller relationship, where sellers must seek to understand the evolving needs of buyers.

Under this premise, the information systems group must be a proactive searcher, aggressively seeking to understand the needs of its internal customers as they occur and, if possible, before they are required. This approach, however, is quite different than has historically been expected of information systems personnel. In fact, the historical profile of an information systems professional is more likely to exclude such responsibilities (for example, selling) being presented in this chapter. Yet, despite differences with historical norms, to be successful information systems departments will either recruit or cultivate such individuals, who are both capable and willing to interact throughout the firm. Developing successful information systems personnel who mingle department-to-department is only the start of the process, however, as it will take time and significant energy to ensure that other departments and personnel believe that the information systems personnel are sincere in meeting their needs. In fact, this process will take a considerable amount of time, as initially there will likely be a great deal of skepticism about these efforts.

MANAGERIAL IMPACTS

Critical to the success of technological synergy is the manner in which information systems personnel are channeled into their external (non-information systems) assignments. To be successful, the placement must be seen by information systems professionals as a positive action, which over the length of the individual's career cultivates positive results. For instance, consider an individual from information systems who is placed in engineering for this type of cross-functional assignment. Subsequently when he or she is promoted at some point, and this promotion is linked formally or informally to the engineering assignment, the benefits of such placements become increasingly visible, which in turn escalates the desirability of such opportunities. In this context, this type usage of information systems personnel will be seen not as punishment but as an opportunity to broaden the expertise, skills, knowledge and understanding of the information systems individual assigned. Hence, this assignment enhances the productivity of the organization and individual.

This approach, therefore, rests on the ability of the organization to demonstrate successfully that these kinds of activities directly enhance the intraorganizational value of the information systems professional. Under this process, the successful integration of technical synergy rests on the abilities and willingness of management formally to migrate information systems personnel throughout the organization.

From a practical standpoint, such assignments will not require the same degree of commitment or time on the part of the information systems professional. As a result, the information system assignments will be in many organizations on both a full-time and part-time basis (clearly the need will not exist for full-time assignments in all cases). In turn, this possibility of such dual assignments (full- and part-time) creates two separate types of considerations for information systems personnel and their respective organization.

Full- and Part-Time Information Systems Personnel Assignments

The largest concern that occurs under both possible situations is the result of full-time assignments being made to departments that are external to the information systems department. Full-time assignments cultivate the greatest dilemma because such duties tend to isolate the assigned information systems professional, keeping him or her removed from the home (information systems) department. Further it is extremely complicated to evaluate the performance of an individual who has been assigned tasks that may fall outside traditional information systems boundaries. Consider for example an auditor being assigned to work full-time in a marketing department. Over time, the auditor loses contact and visibility with his or her departmental counterparts, who later play a critical role in the intra-firm success of this individual. This condition is further complicated because, when assigned full-time to other responsibilities, this individual is easily and often forgotten by home department members, underscoring the attitude that such external assignments are a form of pasturing someone out of the organization. For this reason, it is recommended that full-time assignments of this nature not be utilized except under either the most drastic conditions or only for a short duration.

A different problem that arises out of part-time information systems assignments is that it is often very difficult to assess the quality of the work of the information systems professional. In fact, such assignments are often not quantitatively evaluated, leaving significant questions as to the performance of the individual. Further confused because short-term assignments often decrease the visibility and seeming importance of the assignment, these projects are often seen as a way of giving an individual something to do, which obviously decreases the internal value of the assignment (and in turn, the individual). However, in general and despite the drawbacks, these short-term assignments seem to work best, particularly when the two supervisors (information systems and the other departmental manager) communicate clearly and often as to the performance of the individual. More specifically, the flow of communication within the firm between the information systems department and other functional departments and the immediate supervisors is a critical element in the successful implementation of technological synergy.

Inter-Office Communication Flows

Reasonably, many information systems department heads and other functional managers may suggest that they are currently accomplishing technological synergy through the careful assignment and availability of information systems personnel to specified departments. Thus, one can expect that if queried, most department heads will enforce their professional support and successful work with their information systems department. In contrast, however, we propose that this process requires very specific tasks to ensure the formal linkage between two separate departments. Managers engaged in this process must understand that this is a formal assignment of the information systems professional to a specified department. In other words, the information systems professional assumes a formal reporting and interacting process that is part of his or her annual evaluation. The positive aspect of this approach is that it leaves no question as to the nature of the assignment. That is, the information systems professional is working with another department, and as part of his or her formal annual evaluation, he or she is expected to enrich the performance of that department.

As a result of developing a formal assignment process, the information systems manager, as well as the functional head (where the information systems professional is assigned), must collaborate and work collectively with the other department manager (assessing performance and accomplishments). Failure to have such a communication flow reduces the impact and the strength of implementing technological synergy throughout the firm, as the individual information systems professional will develop few linkages between his or her assignments and the total responsibility of his or her job. For instance, for this process to work effectively, two managers sharing an information systems professional may meet once a month with the information systems staff member to review his or her accomplishments, concerns, progress, and so forth on related assignments. Correspondingly, this outlook assists reaching performance outcomes through the buyer-seller arrangement we proposed earlier in this section. Hence, through the strategic placement of information systems personnel within each department, each specific information systems individual is held formally accountable for the assigned department having their technology needs satisfied.

Future Considerations

As the underlying roles of information systems personnel change, management must closely examine the capabilities of these personnel, as well as the underlying mission of the firm and the departments where information systems personnel will be assigned. In turn, this requires understanding how information systems can become an organizational lubricant, increasing the flow of key information. Hence, managers must constantly examine their status, developing an understanding of what organizational and managerial changes must be made to adjust to this evolution.

9

Resource Expenditure Strategies: Anticipating Future Directions

For top management, one of the greatest challenges of emerging technologies is controlling and managing the resource issues related to investing wisely in such a dynamic market. Given the severity of changes that adopting and competing against new technologies often brings, such new ventures can create significant resource allocation dilemmas that are not easily resolved. For instance, the adoption of each new technology is in essence an investment in a new method of doing business. Improper investments obviously lead to less desirable long-term outcomes.

In essence, investments in new technologies must be visualized as strategic allocations of resources. As a result, anticipating strategic directions of technology requires more then the ability to forecast the technology. Beyond such a basic consideration, management must anticipate strategic movements of technology for the purpose of determining the proper resource allocations, both in terms of intensity (how much) and timing (when). Such forecasting requires a dual understanding, therefore, where trading off high value decisions fosters the expectation of high returns. In contrast, low value decisions cultivate low returns. It is under this premise that the purpose of this chapter is formed. Specifically, this chapter will explore the correlation between investments in technology and rewards.

STRATEGIC AND MANAGERIAL ALLOCATIONS

Initially, management must determine the extent to which the firm is able to invest in technologies. Not easily accomplished, this objective requires the ability to determine where the firm is currently as well as to envision future developments and trends of the organization. Hence, such a resource allocation process is initially cultivated from an understanding of future organizational directions. For instance, if the decision has been made to position the firm as a cash cow, where the purpose is to generate large returns with minimum investments, large investments in technology must be made within the context of this vision.

Accordingly, resource allocation decisions must start with top management and include their vision for the firm. Consider for example, the ease with which a firm could install personal computers with little immediate feedback from top management. The long-term orientation of top management (as opposed to middle managers, who focus on operational issues) allows situations to occur where they may not be involved in such decisions. Particularly a concern in those environments where installations can be implemented incrementally (piecemeal), it is possible to develop and install technologies without correlating these investments with the organizational mission. Failure to include the input of top management provides a restriction on the firm's ability to make significant long-term decisions that benefit the organization. Hence, all initial significant allocation decisions must include direct input from top management.

To be able to address resource decisions there are a number of strategic and managerial steps that are required. The top nine steps in resource allocations of technology are included in Table 9.1 and are identified in more detail in the following discussion.

TOP NINE STEPS IN RESOURCE ALLOCATIONS OF TECHNOLOGY

1. *Assess role of technology.* Ensure that the emerging technologies and organizational mission are consistent. Start with the role and goal of top management and work through each organizational level. This requires long-term assessments under a variety of roles, as well as environmental (for example, competitive) conditions.

2. *Create specific organizational objectives of technology (usually done by middle or upper-middle management).* Create very specific expectations of the technology by functional areas (for example, accounting)

TABLE 9.1
Top Nine Steps in Resource Allocations of Technology

Assess role of technology.
Create specific organizational objective of technology (usually done by middle or
    upper-middle management).
Determine each organizational level, individual, and position involved in the
    adoption and usage of technologies.
Combine organizational and departmental technology missions.
Establish realistic time schedules for the implementation of new technologies.
Estimate equipment cost.
Estimate human cost.
Implement technologies.
Follow-up.

including costs and return on investments. Measure managers by their
ability to accomplish these objectives.

3. *Determine each organizational level, individual, and position
involved in the adoption and usage of technologies.* Identify areas where
the technology is needed immediately, as well as those areas where such
investments are needed in the future. Consult with lower management levels to ensure that recent technological advancements are included in the
assessment. Ensure that mechanisms are developed so that all managerial
levels are kept aware of emerging technologies in their area.

4. *Combine organizational and departmental technology missions.*
Use them as a basis to assess inconsistencies, new investments required,
opportunities, problem areas, personnel demands, and so forth.

5 *Establish realistic time schedules for the implementation of new
technologies.* Include training, technical usage, socialization, and so forth
in the establishment of a time schedule. We have found that a 5:1 rule
comes into play. That is, historically there has been a 5 to 1 ratio between
installation and effective usage. For instance, for every day it takes to
install a new technology, it takes five days to use it effectively. If it takes
30 days to install a technology, this rule contends that it takes 150 days
before overall effective usage occurs. What this means is that as the level
of complexity increases in terms of installation, the level of usage of the
technology is more difficult to achieve. This rule, however, can be overcome. For this reason, the preparation of employees to use any technology is a critical undertaking that should be carefully managed.

Corresponding to the development of a time line, the implementation schedule should represent a realistic view of expected accomplishments. Creating unrealistic time expectations simply ensures that technologies will not be installed and utilized as needed. Instead, users under pressure to implement technologies before they are ready to be properly used will create minimal use operations that satisfy the use of the technology but not to the full potential the technology can provide. As a result, users will typically not seek to expand the applications beyond these minimal levels, finding satisfaction in reduced usage. Consequently, this creates a technological backward multiplier effect, where each additional technology that bridges subsequent technologies (for example, expanding processing speed), makes it more difficult for users to recapture current technological benefits because they are constantly falling behind as they are never using current developments.

6. *Estimate equipment cost.* Whatever amount is estimated will likely not be enough. Especially true in the early stages of the product life cycle (as discussed in other portions of this book), technology leadership is similar to addictive behaviors. It is a very expensive undertaking, and the participation in a leadership role should be done under careful scrutiny.

7. *Estimate human costs.* Include training, socialization time, and any period required by users, technicians, or anyone else involved in the technology to utilize effectively the technology as part of the daily routine. The effects that humans have on interfacing with the technology may well be the greatest obstacles to utilization. Expect human costs to be far more difficult in understanding and assessing. Remember the 5:1 rule, and seek to reduce the ratio of installation to usage time.

8. *Implement technologies.* Technologies are physically implemented.

9. *Follow-up.* After a short period of usage (for example, five days), determine the degree to which the technology is being utilized. Expect underutilization, and be delighted if you get desired or overutilization. In situations where desired or overutilization of technologies exist, try to determine what human factors (the most likely cause) led to this situation. Try to export this human synergy to other places in the firm where the underutilization of technologies exists. Assess the progression toward specific goals for that technology. That is, although full usage may not be possible, require that the users of the technology make specific advancements in the usage of the technology in conjunction with previously established time lines. Continue the follow-up for as long as necessary, ensuring intermediate and long-term follow up periods also exist.

ORGANIZATIONAL CONCERNS

The underlying foundation of this chapter is that top management has two basic cost decisions to make when investing in technologies. These decisions, human and equipment resources, although quite different, cultivate separate organizational investments and expectations. However, it is difficult if not impossible to create a formula process to determine expectations for actual investments.

The real issue here in prediction investment decisions is at what point the firm desires to be with respect to the technologies (for example, leader or follower). This is of course a philosophical and practical decision that must be made at the top of the firm. From this decision, a course of action can be charted for the firm. Without such a decision, it is impossible to create an orderly flow of the adoption and usage of technologies organizationally. There are, however, certain questions top management can ask in determining the technology correspondence between their firm and the adoption of technologies. These questions include the following.

Are we willing to change with every new technology? A commitment to being at the forefront of technological adoption requires constant assessment and adjustment. An unwillingness to make such adjustments suggests a smaller likelihood that significant resource allocation is justified for this organization.

How well have organizational members adapted to new technologies in the past? Understanding the ability of this particular organization to cope with past adoption of new technologies provides a roadmap to the ability to accept changes in the future. Organizations that have adjusted well to new developments are obviously more likely to be better adopters in the future. Correspondingly, this issue can be viewed for both the entire organization and functional areas.

Have significant changes been made since the last technological adoptions? If dramatic changes were made since the last adoptions of new technologies, how will these impact in a positive or negative sense the ability of the organization to adopt new technologies?

Is this technology right for the firm? Not all technologies fit into the scope, direction, and intent of the firm. A decision must be made if a technology is right for the organization. This decision generally falls under the middle management framework and concerns the appropriateness of a technology or family of technologies. Some technologies, for instance, just do not fit into the framework of the organization. Consider the manufacturer who performs inventories for buyers on a systematic basis. Although these inventories can be done electronically (such as consumer goods companies are doing for large retailers through their customer checkout system), there remains a need to have a human relationship between the buyer and seller. For this reason, the utilization of a strictly electronic relationship or interconnection may not be in the best interest of the seller, even though costs could probably be reduced through such a bond. Accordingly, the seller in this and related examples, may find that certain emerging technologies are not a good fit for this situation.

Are we willing to change our minds about adopting technologies? Because a decision must be made regarding technologies, these decisions should not be considered sacred cows without an opportunity to review outcomes. Hence, no decision with respect to technology should be considered final. When a decision is made for the organization and outcomes turn out to be less than expected, there must be a willingness and ability to go in another direction. Having a strictly inflexible decision process guarantees failure, especially since it is often impossible to predict the magnitude and usefulness of technologies. Management must be willing to learn from mistakes and be willing to modify directions when organizational conditions warrant adjustments.

Recognize that technologies come in families. New technologies initially look like single inventions. Over time however, we discover that most new technologies are related to other products and these advancements are usually accompanied by other advancements, both to this product and related products. For this reason, we should consider technologies are part of a family of advancements, many of which we have not seen. Consider the advancements, for instance, that have been ushered in with the personal computer. Developments in printers, video games, cars, phone systems, and so forth have all accompanied the development of personal computers. Organizational managers should be prepared to anticipate future advancements in their resource expenditure strategies.

10

New Technologies:
New Problems and Solutions

The rapid development and integration of technologies within business markets has created a number of problems that are new to the business community. Yet, the development of these new problems has really just begun. As technologies are increasingly expanding their offerings and capabilities, opportunities for outright theft are escalating, cultivating significant problems within the business community. In this vein, the underlying purpose of this chapter is to identify and discuss a number of these major concerns (Table 10.1) coupled with suggested initial solutions. Although this is not meant to be an exhaustive list, it underscores the problems that rapid technological development creates within many business firms.

NON OR LOW-USE OF NEW TECHNOLOGIES

Problem

This can be referred to as a why-bother-to-learn-it philosophy. This philosophy is commonly evident among workers who see their career near its end or for those who are afraid, insecure, and most importantly lack sufficient training in the particular technology. This problem area is one that most managers can easily identify and relate to within their professional experiences. More specifically, this issue deals with the degree to

TABLE 10.1
Problems Associated with New Technologies

Non- or low use of new technologies
Escalating costs
Remaining current
Training and development of employees in technologies
Technology maintenance
Technological Theft
Personal use of technologies on the boss's dime

---

which firms are able to socialize technologies throughout the appropriate organizational levels, with the understanding that all employees do not equally utilize new technologies. In this environment, the purchase of technologies represents one cost issue, and the willingness of employees to utilize these technologies is a second and sometimes a more difficult hurdle.

The non-use problem has always been a major constraint to firms making major changes. As an illustration that is particularly prevalent, consider Table 10.2. In this table, it is illustrated how the adoption of electronic commerce has become an accepted method of exchange by many countries, yet remains a minority system within the United States.

As this table indicates, the availability of a technology, even one that seemingly reduces or minimizes many problems (for example, carrying cash, balancing checkbooks) is not guaranteed to ensure that people will use the technology. In this light however, there are several solutions that can decrease the severity of this situation.

Solution

First, management must make it extremely clear that the use of the specific technology is not a personal choice, but instead a professional requirement. As such, performance linkages will be made to the use of technology that can include, promotions, raises, contests, and so on. Hence, the non- or low using employee is made to understand that there is a personal accountability that is linked to the application of the technology. In this vein, communication is made exceedingly clear to the firm's employees that failure to use the technology will directly generate a number of negative outcomes to the individual employee.

TABLE 10.2

Country Comparison of Check Writing versus Other Payment Methods

Type of Payment	Percentage of Transactions
Paper check	75.0
Credit card	16.0
Electronic	3.0
Debit card	2.6
Wire transfer	0.1

Regional Comparisons of Non-check Usage Per Person

Region	Percentage
Japan	75
Europe	70
Canada	59
United States	25

Source: Lucinda Harper, "Why Americans Just Won't Stop Writing Checks: Electronic Payments Are Viewed as Too Complicated," *The Wall Street Journal*, 102 (November 24, 1998): A2, A6.

Accompanying the first solution, management must ensure that employees receive sufficient training in the use and specific application of any new technologies. This may in some cases require an extensive amount of time devoted to working with employees in developing specific technological applications. The training, therefore, may come in two distinct stages. The first training focuses on the basic use of the technology. That is, the worker is taught about the basic mechanics of how the technology is used. Then in a second stage the employee is prepared in applying the technology to his or her specific job requirements. The first stage may be provided by an in-house technical specialist, but the second stage of training may require that employees in the discipline who already understand the technology work within their functional area as trainers.

ESCALATING COSTS

Problem

The costs of new technology have not and in the future will not go down in a relative sense. New technologies are not relatively inexpensive during their introductory period. That is, new technologies always cost more. It is reasonable, however, to conclude that although the relative costs of technology may show some decline over the next ten years, there is no reason to believe that real costs will decline. Thus, investments in technology can and should be seen as a significant investment that will not experience a real decline.

Solution

There are several views that management can take of this continuing cost. First, management must decide to what degree they desire to be at the leading edge of technology. Under this scenario, all firms do not, must not, and should not acquire technology at the same rate. Consider, for example, an examination of the evolutionary decline of the pricing of personal computers. Shedding light through an understanding of the introduction and maintenance of new products, personal computers typically have a high initial cost, which over a short period falls dramatically. Equally, products that have been in the marketplace a short period often experience rapid price reductions. Thus, although it may be exciting to have new technologies, not being at the beginning of the technology curve does not always provide a significant disadvantage, as the high acquisition costs can overshadow advantages. In fact, like most technologies, the initial costs of securing products are high, as providers try to reacquire investment costs rapidly. For this reason, if no immediate advantage is provided through the rapid acquisition of technology, top management may delay technological acquisitions until they have been available within the marketplace for a period of time.

At the basis of this reasoning, it is understood that some firms constantly need to spend more in current dollars to remain competitive through technologies. Thus, their success is based upon the strategic usage of technology that must be maintained. Of course, in this environment there is no choice but to invest in technologies early in their product life cycle, even at a very high cost. To accomplish organizational goals under the setting that the firm must be technologically superior, management must adopt a basic viewpoint or perspective that accepts that new technologies are critical to the success of the firm and they must be possessed. Management must understand its technology perspective and assess the costs in that light.

REMAINING CURRENT

Problem

As technologies change, it is always difficult to keep up with contemporary innovations. Even in those organizations that are committed financially to having the latest technology, currency is an extremely difficult task that can be overwhelming. When one considers the large number of changes and investments that are required for a firm to remain current technologically (training of technical and nontechnical personnel, financial resources, ability to secure sufficient numbers of the new technologies, integrating the technologies within the firm, and so forth), opportunities are very limited.

Solution

Remaining current basically requires two dependent activities, both of which are controlled directly and indirectly by top management. First, resources must be made available to secure necessary technological products and associated expenses (for example, training of personnel). The financial aspect of remaining current represents a difficult challenge for many organizations, although it is an activity that must be anticipated accurately if the strategic goal is to be a technology leader.

The second component, however, of remaining technologically current is a more difficult challenge because it focuses on the human aspect of technology interacting with employees. More specifically, organizations desiring to remain at the forefront of technology are signaling that they have committed their personnel to being able to work with and apply tools that are at the beginning of the technology product life cycle. It is useless to have new technologies that cannot be used. This philosophy requires a very significant understanding of the type of personnel who are comfortable, and indeed enjoy, the rigors of working with unknown technologies. As we have noted previously this can be a problem, as all individuals do not enjoy working with new innovations. The evidence of this condition is everywhere, as we see that new products of all types are usually slow to gain marketplace acceptance. Even those products that offer clear advantages are often slow to gain initial acceptance as consumers display reluctance and constant uneasiness at purchasing new products. Hence, it is clear that not all individuals are suited to working in an environment where the socialization of employees to new technologies occurs systematically and consistently.

To install current technologies successfully, the firm must be able to understand and identify the professional and personal qualities on the part of employees that reflect a willingness to accept and use new products. To accomplish this goal may require a reexamination of current employment practices, ensuring that specific guidelines that identify such traits are available to hiring managers.

TRAINING AND DEVELOPMENT OF EMPLOYEES IN TECHNOLOGIES

Problem

The mere acquisition of technologies within the firm is seldom sufficient. This is because employees must be able to understand how the technologies should be used within the framework of their specific job position. The challenge of this problem, therefore, is to construct an organization that has the ability to utilize acquired technologies.

Solution

Training and development represent separate activities, particularly as they relate to technologies. More specifically, training represents skill or knowledge presentation for the purpose of an immediate increase in abilities. Development, in contrast, represents a long-term outlook, where the individual is provided information, skills, and so forth that over a long period (for example, several years) are expected to make changes in behaviors.

Training of personnel in technologies is, in general, considerably easier than development. Accordingly, the training of personnel in technologies represents a significant human resource commitment, although this commitment can often be very short term in nature. As a result, many organizations now rely upon the successful outsourcing of training personnel in technologies. Consider, for example, the large number of entrepreneurial firms that will come to your office and train your employees in the utilization of new software.

Done in the proper setting by the correct training professionals, outsourcing technological training can be a successful venture. Typically, of course, smaller firms are more likely to outsource training, and larger organizations are more likely to train internally. The advantage of training is that while top management must anticipate such programs in advance, this planning can often be limited to a specified period of time.

In contrast to training, the development of personnel in using contemporary technologies represents a long-term effort that is never completed (because technologies are constantly revised, personnel development accompanies technological updating). In this environment, planning becomes a critical element, as plans are constructed to mold personnel strategically to a specific framework. Hence, development represents a more strategic outlook than training. For this reason, the development aspect of preparing personnel to fit into strategic molds is a much more difficult task. Consider, for example, that the fluidness of the environment makes it extremely difficult to predict accurately where technologies are headed, both within the context of their level and when this level of sophistication will occur.

Therefore, successful employee technology development will have to be seen as a strategic entity. That is, formal plans will have to be constructed and evaluated on an annual basis that are designed to extend over several years. In many cases this suggests that a single organizational member must be held responsible for the long-term progress of personnel activities that relate to technology adoption and usage. In turn, the success for such plans (and the individual) must be measured systematically and formally. This plan should include an assessment of current personnel, both by position and name, expectations of evolving technologies and how they will influence these individuals and their positions, training requirements by position and specific individual, personnel, and time tables for these evolutions.

TECHNOLOGY MAINTENANCE

Problem

As with any evolving process, there is a need to maintain the level of abilities of the technology to fulfill the assigned tasks. Because of the increasingly complex nature of many technologies, it is extremely difficult to be able to retain their current efficiency level.

Solution

There are two basic solutions for maintaining technologies. The first potential solution is to have internal employees who will take care of problems. This solution offers a variety of benefits if the organization is large enough to create economies of scale with respect to maintenance. In contrast, however, the second potential solution is outsourcing, where maintenance is all done externally.

Our suggestion is when possible, consider minimally that although both internal and external maintenance must be performed, the goal here is to be strategically sufficient. Thus, we are suggesting that when possible, consider some internal support, even if minimal. Of course, although size and resources often dictate the ability of a firm to perform maintenance, consider an example that we noted several years ago, that underscores the simplicity of internally maintaining some technologies.

We had a business associate who ran a small interconnect phone business, selling new phone equipment and installations. Over several years, he had returned a number of products to manufacturers because of equipment malfunctions. Curious as to the nature of the maintenance being performed, he opened up a fairly complex phone system, and traced invisible ink over the internal parts before he returned the system to the manufacturer to be repaired. When the phone system was returned, he simply reexamined the parts and determined what had been replaced (it is important to note that he was not even minimally technically skilled). Doing this same activity a number of times over a year, he concluded that in the majority of cases the same part was being replaced, which required no technical skill. He then found a vendor who would sell that part for a very low price. Hence, when equipment was returned for repair, he would always have that part removed first to determine if it was the offending part. If the part were the cause of the problem, he would replace it, return the phone, and bill the customer. If the part was not malfunctioning, he simply sent the entire phone system on to the repair shop. In a very short period of time, this individual had built a very successful and profitable repair business based on limited technical skills and knowledge about phone systems.

From this example, we are illustrating that simple maintenance can sometimes be done internally, even when no repair facilities or experts are available. It is our contention that as technologies become increasingly more complex, it is beneficial to train some personnel in very basic troubleshooting. The savings in money and time can be staggering. For example, the time and cost to send a secretary to a program that trains in troubleshooting computers is very low. In turn, the company secures an individual who is around most of the time, probably spends lots of time on the personal computer anyway, and is capable of solving small problems at a very low cost. Our experience is also that being placed in such a position of being able to offer additional help to other organizational members adds value to the individual's job.

TECHNOLOGICAL THEFT

Problem

The rapid growth of technologies has opened up a new industry of technological theft and destruction, much of which we suspect has not been discovered or controlled. The history of technologies, particularly in recent times, suggests that as new tools are ushered quickly into business organizations, a small number of individuals look for loopholes to use the new products for personal profit. For example, the rapid integration of information technologies on accessible communication lines (for example, modems) has opened up new opportunities for these people we often refer to as hackers. Although some of these hackers seek to put money directly into their pockets, others are trying to enter illegally into corporate communication channels simply to see if they can intercede into these systems. Further, hackers often include existing employees who simply wander the communication lines, curious as to what they can find of interest. Yet, even in these cases where there is no intent of malice, such activities cannot be allowed to continue. Given that the purpose in all these cases is to profit somehow (monetary or personal pleasure profit motives), these individuals must be considered as technology thieves who threaten the existence of business firms.

Solution

Technological theft is very difficult to anticipate. Further, although we are hesitant to recommend that management assume that some individuals will take advantage of technologies, the fact is this seems always to be true. That is, as technologies advance, the assumption always has to be that there are people who will seek out ways to use those technologies to advance their agendas, even when to do so is illegal or immoral. Hence, our suggestion is that several steps always be taken with respect to the introduction of new technologies. Although there are other considerations beyond what we present here, and we do not consider this an all-inclusive list, it is our recommendation that these and other related issues be addressed by top management.

First, management must accept that any new technologies provide opportunities for exploitation. To reduce these conditions, it is necessary first to assess these potential opportunities and be willing to make corrections, limitations, restrictions, or any other steps that will minimize the potential for exploitation. Notice that we are not saying that a proactive process will eliminate these opportunities, as that is extremely unlikely under most conditions. To accomplish this task, ensure that internal expertise is sufficient to assess these potentials, and when not, aggressively employ external professionals as part of a routine review of safeguards.

Second, through close work with internal technical employees, systematically employ external experts who are constantly assessing the progress of such exploitations of such advancements with the sole purpose of assessing risks and finding theft. This may include, for example, a yearly technological audit with a strong focus on assessing risks and discovering abuses.

Third, develop a rigorous hiring process that places technical employees who have the potential to exploit the system under a higher degree of scrutiny than other, less exposed employees.

THE PERSONAL USE OF TECHNOLOGIES ON THE BOSS'S DIME

Problem

Most agree that excessive use of technologies including Internet use is a problem that is growing as fast as the Web itself. The personal use of business assets has always been a problem, with many corporations finding such behaviors resulting in an excessive loss of firm resources. On a very basic level, consider the employee who uses the office copier to make duplicates of personal tax forms. Given the common occurrence of this event around mid-April in many offices, it is evident that consistent with these actions, we generally operate in an environment where such behaviors are tolerated, at least somewhat.

Although it should be noted that these behaviors are usually not meant to cause problems, they foster a real economic drain on the firm. In this environment, it is evident that employees to a very large extent have been given free rein with a high degree of immunity in the general use of business resources.

Personal use of technologies may fall into this same category. Employees who use the Web excessively often do so at work, spending a third or more of their day surfing or chatting. There is a form of hypnotic effect of staring at a screen. When color, movement, sound, endless availability of information, and instantaneous responses are added it is a potent and seductive distraction to employees.

We propose it is the careful management of critical areas that can be most effectively managed. In this light, firms must determine what technological resources are most critical and in turn how they should be managed most effectively.

Solution

For instance, the use of personal computers to play different kinds of computer games has become a significant problem in some organizations. We know of one organization where every week during the winter, a golf tournament is held within a department. Department members play the game and record the results. Technologies that are most likely to be misused internally are often those that offer entertainment value. Hence, if a new technology is provided an office, and the technology does not offer immediate entertainment value, the misuse will be less than in cases where the offering is fun to use. This is because doing fun things has always been a diversion, and in the context of technologies this will not change. In contrast, those technologies that either do or can generate fun are more likely to be misused. With all these actions taking place on the premise of the business organization (playing the game, posting scores, and so forth), it is fair to say that productivity would be reduced during key matches and tournaments.

To minimize the personal use of technologies in the office, it is important initially to understand how the individual employee views the technology. That is, does the technology seem to induce productivity, or do those most interested in its use have no clear understanding of how the technology can and should be used in the firm? In this environment, therefore, we are noting that it is a lack of clear understanding of the technology within the context of an individualized position where problems may develop. Thus, the critical aspect of minimizing personal use is the degree to which each employee is trained as to its use. The more direct benefits and explanations that employees receive on the technology, coupled with a sense of responsibility and supervision in some cases, the less likely they are to use it inappropriately. Corresponding to this training, therefore, is the degree to which employees receive direct instructions as to how the technology can and should be used.

We are not saying, however, that before a new technology is introduced it should face the litmus test as to whether it offers employees fun. That is, should a firm restrict the use of technologies to those that clearly present no potential for enjoyment? No, we are proposing that as part of the process of the introduction of new technologies, an overt attempt should be made to make management aware of the potential for entertainment distractions on some technologies. This, however, can also present a positive condition in certain situations. That is, it is conceivable for such activities to foster a sort of team environment, where the personal use of these technologies enhances the attractiveness of a job. For instance, the personal use of e-mail to communicate with distant relatives offers a great number of benefits to both the individual and indirectly through good will the firm. In our previous example where departmental members played computer golf, we noticed that over time the employees who participated seemed to exhibit higher levels of trust, cooperation, and communication than existed among non-playing employees.

Research about Internet behavior is ongoing and should be considered by managers as the Internet with its boundarylessness has the potential to suck you in for long periods of time. Managers must account for the reductions of productivity as employees develop cases of Internetamania.

11

Conclusions:
Opportunities and
Risks of Technologies

The rapid evolution of technologies into business markets has provided a host of new opportunities for business firms while simultaneously elevating the level of risk to most organizations. In this setting, embracing technologies carries rewards that can be significant (for example, expanding the abilities of employees), as well as the cultivation of destructive risk to the firm (for example, theft through technology), much of which is unpredictable. For example, as enhanced teleconferencing is provided to regional sales managers, these enrichments will theoretically improve the capabilities of sales managers (for example, regularly meet with superiors and subordinates), as well as the firm, other internal managers, and employees in their internal and external networks. Yet, despite the advent of many advantages, the introduction of such advancements comes with a direct cost to the firm. For example, how much money will the initial teleconferencing cost? Further, as this technology becomes dated, what will be the impact on the firm and employees who have used this equipment? Will managers, for instance, be able to change their habits, dropping the use of familiar technologies and embracing the usage of new tools as they replace old ones? Will firms be able and willing to make the necessary resource commitments to maintain a similar high level of technological competence? In a setting such as this, it is apparent that something as basic as the dating of technology fosters significant long-term impacts on organizational effectiveness, cultivating positive and negative outcomes.

Thus, the application of technology often creates a wide wake, cultivating numerous implications that must be independently assessed. In this vein, we offer several key issues for users to ponder as part of their consideration and acceptance of new business technologies.

THE ENVIRONMENT

Technological investments typically occur in an environment where it is difficult to assess the direct contributions of technology to performance. This void occurs because technology advances at an increasing rate. Consequently, technological assessment measures are often created after the technology has become obsolete, or the assumption is made that the technology advances the cause of the firm with no specific proof being offered. As a result, top management in leading edge, technologically driven firms must accept that they often have to make decisions that cannot be easily assessed or evaluated in a timely fashion. In essence, the measurement of success is often based on a feeling of contribution, which is clearly not a comfortable consideration when we are talking about millions of dollars.

PREDICTING TECHNOLOGICAL ADVANCEMENTS

Accurately forecasting the state of any single line of technology is extremely difficult. A successful technological adapter is one who utilizes technology to maximize a competitive advantage. It requires the ability to anticipate such developments as a critical foundation of success.

There is no absolute success formula here, although it is interesting to note that a constant review of existing literature often provides a basis of forecasting. Coupled with having contact with manufacturers who have constructed a business out of forging technology into their business offerings hastens success in the forecasting of change. That is, we propose that those who are successful are often not those who identify technology first, but the users who are knowledgeable enough to recognize the potential of these benefits in an early stage of introduction.

BE A WILLING ADAPTER

As with the adoption or usage of any new product, a number of variables impact an organization's ability to accept new concepts. Yet, we believe that for technology specifically, it is the attitude of the users and their organizations that dictates the degree to which adaptation is possible.

In this vein, management must construct a firm that is in essence composed of willing adapters. Hence, the recruitment and retention of individuals who are willing to try and accept new ventures underscore the degree to which new technologies can and will be accepted. To reach this goal, management must ensure that mechanisms are in place corporate wide that embrace this attitude.

EXAMINE SUCCESSFUL AND UNSUCCESSFUL RECRUITMENT STRATEGIES

Because so much emphasis is placed on the merging of technology with employees, top management must examine the degree to which technology and employees can be mutually directed. Of course in most cases, for a single firm to control the growth of technology is impossible. However, the selection of employees is a critical activity that can and should be carefully managed in conjunction with the growth of technologies. In this vein, we propose that management examine those strategies that have produced employees who are technically competent within the parameters and demands of the firm. For instance, universities have historically had varying degrees of success in producing technically skilled employees. Because of the nature of academia (tenured professors, expense of securing new technologies, high degree of bureaucratic structure, wide range of student admittance policies, etc.), management should not expect universities to turn out the same quality of new employee consistently. Accordingly, management should systematically assess the degree to which this or any other given source (or strategy) satisfies organizational requirements for providing employees a consistent level of technical competency.

TECHNOLOGY AUDIT

Management should undergo on a regular basis an internal audit to establish where the firm is technologically and where it will be in the future. Only through a systematic examination of expected versus actual levels of adopted technology can strategic improvements be made to the levels of technology utilized. In this vein, it should not be assumed that all new technologies mutually benefit every firm. Each technology, particularly those high in resource commitments, should be systematically examined to assess the degree to which it contributes to the success of the firm's mission. Those that fail the contribution factor should be expelled, or better yet, never accepted. Equally, those technologies that do make a major contribution should be willingly accepted.

A STRATEGIC DECISION

Adopting, utilizing, or even avoiding technologies must be seen as strategic management decisions. Similar to decisions to engage in other actions (revenue producing, positioning, etc.), the integration of technology embraces a number of key resources that require the commitment of top management. Therefore, in some organizations this requires a reexamination of the managerial (personnel) structures that oversee technological development. For instance, the development of new positions (for example, manager of strategic technology) that embrace such a perspective provides both an acknowledgement of such a philosophical outlook and a mechanism for preparing for future evolutions.

RESOURCE COMMITMENTS

Technology is a very expensive endeavor. Firms desiring to utilize this tool successfully to gain a competitive advantage need to establish expenditure levels that are satisfactory with top management as well as consistent with internal management practices and intentions.

MEASURING TECHNOLOGY'S SUCCESS

Organizations typically assess the degree to which individual inputs contribute to organizational success. For instance, salespeople and their managers are generally evaluated on their ability to generate sales. Consistent with this approach, most firms expect to evaluate the degree to which individuals, organizations, and actions are successful. Yet, how do we measure the impact of personal computers within the work force? Generally we do not. Instead we accept the notion that such tools engender overall success, although exact measurements are usually left to speculation. Therefore, it is our view that there will always be difficulty in assessing the direct impact of technology on the work force. Still, this does not mean management should accept a non-assessment outlook. Instead, other tools can be designed internally that provide a basis of initial and ongoing assessment (for example, qualitative interviews) that at least minimally measure levels of accomplishment. Over time, these internal tests should become more stringent, although it is likely management must accept that exact tools for measurement will always lag new technologies.

CONCLUSION

We remind managers that technologies have always offered a competitive advantage to those who properly utilize these resources. There is little question in a practical sense as to the truth of this issue. That is, it is a general tenet that when technologies are properly managed they will provide users significant competitive advantages. For this reason, we think it is appropriate to warn readers that not all technologies fit within the structure of the firm. Importantly, once significant decisions are made to invest in such resources, it often becomes impossible to deviate rapidly from this course of action. Consider the very long time it takes for a large passenger ship to turn around in the ocean. Correspondingly, businesses often take very long periods to make internal changes once commitments are made to invest in technologies, particularly if these technologies are not a match for the mission of the firm.

The key, of course, is to balance the usage of technologies, finding the right level of application without overextending the firm and its resources. For example, in smaller firms overextending the ability of the organization to make reasonable technological commitments is easily done because of the persuasive management style of most owners or presidents. If the owner or president of a small firm becomes absorbed in a new technology, this personal desire can be forced down through the entire firm, despite the fact that there may not be a strong need for these technologies. Thus, the business may be required to take on a technology that is not appropriate for the firm, the employees, or their mission. Despite the potential for this to occur and the dangers it embraces, when significant imbalances do occur in small firms they are often noticed quickly because of the physical proximity workers often have to each other and the ease with which management often notices changes in productivity in smaller organizations.

Long-term and significant mismatching of technologies and the mission of the firm, however, is more likely to occur in larger organizations. When the absorption of new technologies can be overlooked until the cost has multiplied far beyond reasonable levels (such as can occur in larger firm because of bureaucracies), bigger organizations tend to lose track of their missions, correspondingly relinquishing the rationale for initially adopting the technologies. Hence, the need to assess and evaluate the level of what is needed versus what can be afforded is an ongoing question that can never be totally assessed. That is, the need to evaluate continually the conditions of what internally exists and what technologies are needed is critical, although particularly difficult in larger firms. For this reason, it is our concluding position that the assessment of technologies must be an ongoing process, and successful users will understand and apply this concept.

References

Alderson, W. (1965), *Dynamic Marketing Behavior*. Homewood, IL: Irwin.

Alderson, W. (1957), *Marketing Behavior and Executive Action*. Homewood, IL: Irwin.

Anders, George (1998), "Internet Advertising, Just Like Its Medium, Is Pushing Boundaries," *The Wall Street Journal*, 102 (November 30), A1–A6.

Anderson, Erin and Barton Weitz (1992), "The Use of Pledges to Build and Sustain Commitment in Distribution Channels," *Journal of Marketing Research*, 29 (February), 18–34.

Anderson, James C., Hakan Hakansson, and Jan Johanson (1994), "Dyadic Business Relationships within a Business Network Context," *Journal of Marketing*, 58 (October), 1–15.

Apte, U., C. S. Sankar, M. Thakur, and J. E. Turner (1990), "Reusability-Based Strategy for Development of Information Systems: Implementation Experience of a Bank," *MIS Quarterly*, 14 (December), 421–33.

Bagozzi, Richard P. (1975), "Marketing as Exchange," *Journal of Marketing*, 39 (October), 32–39.

Baldwin, Dick (1997), "Wood Supply Changes Certain in 21st Century," *Wood Technology*, 124 (March), 28–40.

Ballantine, John W., Frederick W. Cleveland, and C. Timothy Koeller (1993), "Profitability, Uncertainty, and Firm Size," *Small Business Economics*, 5 (June), 87–100.

Bartlett, Christopher A. and Sumantra Goshal (1996), "Release the Entrepreneurial Hostages from Your Corporate Hierarchy," *Strategy & Leadership*, 24 (July-August), 36–42.

Basalla, George (1989), *The Evolution of Technology.* New York: Cambridge University Press.

Baxter, Leslie A. and Eric P. Simon (1993), "Relationship Maintenance Strategies and Dialectical Contradictions in Personal Relationships," *Journal of Social and Personal Relationships,* 10 (May), 225–42.

Benton, Alberto M. and Glen L. Gray (1993), "Managerial and Technical Factors Related to Strategic Impact of Information Technology," *Journal of Information Technology Management,* 4, 15–27.

Bergeron, Francois and Louis Raymond (1992), "Planning of Information Systems To Gain a Competitive Edge," *Journal of Small Business Management,* 30 (January), 21–26.

Bharadwaj, Sundar G., P. Rajan Varadarajan, and John Fahy (1993), "Sustainable Competitive Advantage in Service Industries: A Conceptual Model and Research Propositions," *Journal of Marketing,* 57 (October), 83–99.

Bloom, Paul N., George R. Milne, and Robert Adler (1994), "Avoiding Misuse of New Information Technologies: Legal and Societal Considerations," *Journal of Marketing,* 58 (January), 98–110.

Brandt, S.C. (1986), *Entrepreneuring in Established Companies,* Homewood, IL: Dow Jones-Irwin.

Brooks, Rick (1999), "Alienating Customers Isn't Always a Bad Idea, Many Firms Discover," *The Wall Street Journal,* 103 (January 7), A1, A12.

Carland, J. A., F. Hoy, and A. C. Carland (1988), "Who Is an Entrepreneur? Is the Wrong Question," *Entrepreneurship: Theory and Practice,* 13 (Fall), 33–39.

Cespedes, Frank V. (1996), *Managing Marketing Linkages.* Upper Saddle River, NJ: Prentice-Hall.

Child, J. (1972), "Organization Structure, Environment, and Performance: The Role of Strategic Choice," *Sociology,* 6 (January), 1–22.

Churchill, Gilbert A. and J. Paul Peter (1995), *Marketing Creating Value for Customers.* Burr Ridge, IL: Austen Press.

Churchill, Neil C. and Daniel F. Muzyka (1994), "Defining and Conceptualizing Entrepreneurship: A Process Approach," in Gerald E. Hills, (Ed.), *Marketing and Entrepreneurship: Research Ideas and Opportunities,* pp. 11–23. Westport, CT: Quorum Books.

Clark, J. M. (1954), "Competition and the Objectives of Government Policy," in E. Chamberlin (Ed.), *Monopoly and Competition and Their Regulation,* pp. 317–37. London: Macmillan.

Coviello, Nicole (1996), "Foreign Market Entry and Internationalization: The Case of Datacom Software Research," *Entrepreneurship: Theory and Practice,* 20 (Summer), 95–105.

Cuneo, Alice Z. (1995), "Kodak's New Vision," *Advertising Age,* 66 (April 3), 38.

Czajkiewicz, Zbigniew J. and Tomasz R. Wielicki (1994), "CIM-A Journey to Manufacturing Excellence," *Computers & Industrial Engineering,* 27

(September), 91–93.

Damore, Kelley (1995), "NECT Hones Product Line, Gains Ground in U.S. Market," *Computer Reseller News*, (July 24), 81.

David, Fred R., John A. Pearce, and W. Alan Randolph (1989), "Linking Technology and Structure to Enhance Group Performance," *Journal of Applied Psychology*, 74 (April), 233–41.

Davis, Fred D., Richard P. Bagozzi, and Paul R. Warshaw (1992), "Extrinsic and Intrinsic Motivation To Use Computers in the Workplace," *Journal of Applied Social Psychology*, 22, 1111–32.

Day, George S. and Prakash Nedungadi (1994), "Managerial Representations of Competitive Advantage," *Journal of Marketing*, 58 (April), 31–44.

Deeter-Schmelz, Dawn R. and Rosemary Ramsey (1995), "A Conceptualization of the Functions and Roles of Formalized Selling and Buying Teams," *Journal of Personal Selling & Sales Management*, 15 (Spring), 47–60.

DeLone, William H. and Ephraim R. McLean (1992), "Information Systems Success: The Quest for the Dependent Variable," *Information Systems Research*, 3 (March), 60–94.

DeSanctis, Gerardine and Brad M. Jackson (1994), "Coordination of Information Technology Management: Team-based Structures and Computer-based Communication Systems," *Journal of Management Information Systems*, 10 (Spring), 85–110.

Dyer, Robert F. (1987), "An Integrated Design For Personal Computers In the Marketing Curriculum," *Journal of the Academy of Marketing Science*, 15 (Summer), 16–24.

El-Ansary, Adel I., Noel B. Zabriskie, and John M. Browning (1993), "Sales Teamwork: A Dominant Strategy for Improving Sales Force Effectiveness," *Journal of Business and Industrial Marketing*, 8(3), 65–72.

Fefer, Mark D. (1997), "Is Seattle the Next Silicon Valley?" *Fortune*, 136 (July 7), 78–80.

Fleming, Martin (1997), "The New Business Cycle: The Impact of the Application and Production of Information Technology on U.S. Macroeconomic Stabilization," *Business Economics*, 32 (October), 36–42.

Frankwick, Gary L., James C. Ward, Michael D. Hutt, and Peter H. Reingen (1994), "Evolving Patterns of Organizational Beliefs in the Formation of Strategy," *Journal of Marketing*, 58 (April), 96–110.

Ganesan, Shankar (1994), "Determinants of Long-Term Orientation in Buyer-Seller Relationships," *Journal of Marketing*, 58 (April), 119.

Gattuso, Greg (1994), "Kiosks Build Mall Loyalty and Database," *Direct Marketing*, 57 (October), 26–27.

Gillooly, Brian (1994), "IBM Creates Team To Better Manage PS/2, Value-Point," *Computer Reseller News*, (January 17), 2.

Goddard, Sarah (1997), "Picture of Risk, Business Changing," *Business Insurance*, 31 (April 7), 25, 29.

Good, David J. and Robert W. Stone (1995), "Computer Technology and the

Marketing Organization: An Empirical Investigation," *Journal of Business Research*, 34 (November), 197–209.

Good, David J. and Roberta J. Schultz (1997), "Technological Teaming as a Marketing Strategy," *Industrial Marketing Management*, 26 (September), 413–22.

Goodhue, Dale L. and Ronald L. Thompson. (1995), "Task-Technology Fit and Individual Performance." *MIS Quarterly*, 19 (June), 213–36.

Goslar, Martin D. (1987), "Marketing and the Adoption of Microcomputers: An Application of Diffusion Theory," *Journal of The Academy of Marketing Science*, 15 (Summer), 42–48.

Gremillion, Jeff (1997), "Can Smaller Niches Bring Riches?" *Mediaweek*, 7 (October 20), 50–51.

Guimaraes, Tor, Magid Igbaria, and Ming-te Lu (1992), "The Determinants of DSS Success: An Integrated Model," *Decision Sciences*, 23 (March-April), 409–30.

Gundlach, Gregory T. and Patrick E. Murphy (1993), "Ethical and Legal Foundations of Relational Marketing Exchanges," *Journal of Marketing*, 57 (October), 35–46.

Hamlin, Cole (1994), "Team Building a Global Team at Apple Computer," *Employment Relations Today*, 21 (Spring), 55–62.

Hansen, Paul G. (1994), "Getting Your Team on the Same Side," *Financial Executive Magazine* (March-April), 43–49.

Harper, Lucinda (1998), "Why Americans Just Won't Stop Writing Checks: Electronic Payments Are Viewed as Too Complicated," *The Wall Street Journal*, 102 (November 24), A2, A6.

Hartman, Sandra, Olof Lundberg, Michael White, and Tim Barnett (1995), "Information Processing Techniques in Planning: An Investigation of Preferences of Executive Planners," *Journal of Business Research*, 33 (May), 13–34.

Hays, Laurie (1994), "Mental Block," *The Wall Street Journal Reports*, 75 (June 27), R6.

Heide, Jan B. and Allen M. Weiss (1995), "Vendor Consideration and Switching Behavior for Buyers in High-Technology Markets," *Journal of Marketing*, 59 (July), 30–43

Hise, Richard T. and Edward L. Reid (1994), "Improving the Performance of the Industrial Sales Force in the 1990s." *Industrial Marketing Management*, 23 (October), 273–79.

Jessup, Leonard M. and Joseph S. Valacich (1993), *Group Support Systems: New Perspectives*, New York: Macmillan.

Katzenbach, Jon R. and Douglas K. Smith (1993), *The Wisdom of Teams*, Boston, MA: Harvard Business School Press.

Keefe, Thomas and Donald E. Maypole, (Eds.) (1983), "The Future of Practice Relationships," *Relationships in Social Service Practice: Context and Skills*, pp. 233–43. Monterey, CA: Brooks/Cole.

Kiechel, Walter III (1994), "A Manager's Career in the New Economy," *Fortune*, 129 (April 4), 68–72.

Koreto, Richard J. (1996), "Small Firms Can Do Big Business Online," *Journal of Accountancy*, 182 (October), 79–82.

Kotler, Philip (1972), "A Generic Concept of Marketing," *Journal of Marketing*, 36 (April), 46–54.

Kraemer, Kenneth L., Jason Dedrick, Chin-Yeong Hwang, Tze-Chen Tu, and Chee-Sing Yap (1996), "Entrepreneurship, Flexibility, and Policy Coordination: Taiwan's Computer Industry," *Information Society*, 12 (July-September), 215–49.

Krajewski, Steve (1994), "Barnhart Kicks Off Ad Effort To Boost U.S. Olympic Festival," *Adweek*, 16 (December 5), 12.

Kramer, R. and B. Grossman (1987), "Contracting for Social Services: Process Management and Resource Dependencies," *Social Service Review*, 61, 32–55.

Kramer, Scott (1998), "Net Sales," *Golf Magazine* 5 (December), 86–87.

Kurtz, David L. and Louis E. Boone (1987), "The Current Status of Microcomputer Usage in the Marketing Programs of AACSB-accredited Colleges and Universities," *Journal of the Academy of Marketing Science*, 15 (Summer), 10–15.

Lucas, Allison (1994), "Albermarle Increases Stake in Sodium Bromide," *Chemical Week*, 155 (November 16), 9.

Lumpkin, G. T. and Gregory G. Dess (1996), "Clarifying the Entrepreneurial Orientation Construct and Linking It to Performance," *Academy of Management Review*, 21 (January), 135–72.

Manz, Charles C. and Henry P. Sims (1993), *Business Without Bosses*, New York: John Wiley & Sons.

Matthews, Charles H., Xiaodong Quin, and Geralyn McClure Franklin (1996), "Stepping Toward Prosperity: The Development of Entrepreneurial Ventures in China and Russia," *Journal of Small Business Management*, 34 (July), 75–85.

McDowell, Bill (1994), "The Megabyte Bistro," *Restaurants & Institutions*, 104 (September 15), 118–23.

McKee, Daryl and P. Rajan Varadarajan (1995), "Special Issue on Sustainable Competitive Advantage," *Journal of Business Research*, 33 (June), 77–79.

Meeks, Fleming and Dana Wechsler Linden (1994), "Trickle Down Bosses," *Forbes*, 154 (November), 206–10.

Mikalachki, Alexander (1994), "Creating a Winning Team," *Business Quarterly*, 58 (Summer), 14–22.

Miller, D. (1983), "The Correlates of Entrepreneurship in Three Types of Firms," *Management Science*, 29 (July), 770–91.

Monaghan, Robert (1995), "Customer Management Teams Are Here To Stay," *Marketing News*, 29 (November 6), 4.

Montgomery, Barbara M. (1993), "Relationship Maintenance Versus Relationship Change: A Dialectical Dilemma," *Journal of Social and Personal Relationships*, 10 (May), 205–23.

Morley, Dick (1996), "When Products Ruled the Earth . . . ," *Manufacturing Systems*, 14 (February), 84.

Morris, Michael H. and Donald L. Sexton (1996), "The Concept of Entrepreneurial Intensity: Implications for Company Performance," *Journal of Business Research*, 36 (May), 5–13.

Morris, Michael H. and J. D. Trotter (1990), Institutionalizing Entrepreneurship in a Large Company: A Case Study at A.T.& T.," *Industrial Marketing Management*, 19 (May), 131–39.

Murray, Joseph W. (1998), "What Happens if you Don't Implement SFA?" *Sales and Field Force Automation*, 5 (December), 50–54.

Myers, David W. (1995), "Getting Connected: Large and Small Firms Alike Will Need To Embrace These New Technology Standards." *Commercial Investment Real Estate Journal*, 14 (November–December), 21–25.

Nelson, Scott (1998), "Tomorrow's Technology: Marketing," *Forbes*, 1(September), 8.

Nikiforuk, Andrew (1996), "The Amazing Job-creating Machine No One Wants," *Canadian Business*, 69 (June), 205.

Norman, Roy P. (1995), Becoming Information-technology Visionaries," *Financial Executive*, 11 (September–October), 1.

O'Callaghan, Ramon, Patrick J. Kaufmann, and Benn R. Konsynski (1992), "Adoption Correlates and Share Effects of Electronic Data Interchange Systems in Marketing Channels," *Journal of Marketing*, 56 (April), 45–56.

Oliver, Richard L. and Erin Anderson (1994), "An Empirical Test of the Consequences of Behavior- and Outcome-based Sales Control Systems," *Journal of Marketing*, 58 (October), 53–67.

Olson, Eric M., Orville C. Walker, and Robert W. Ruekert (1995), "Organizing for Effective New Product Development: The Moderating Role of Product Innovativeness," *Journal of Marketing*, 59 (January), 48–62.

Opper, Susanna and Henry Fersko-Weiss (1992), *Technology for Teams: Enhancing Productivity in Networked Organizations*, New York: Van Nostrand Reinhold.

O'Reilly, Brian (1994), "Reengineering the MBA," *Fortune*, 129 (January 24), 38–47,

Parker, Glenn M. (1994), *Cross-functional Teams*, San Francisco, CA: Jossey-Bass.

Petersen, Donald and John Hillkirk (1991), *Teamwork: New Management Ideas for the 90s*, London: Victor Gollancz.

Pillsbury, Dennis (1997), "Restoring Entrepreneurship to the Independent Agency System: New Jersey Agency Provides Market Access to Smaller Agencies," *Rough Notes*, 140 (March), 12–14.

Pinchot, G. (1985), *Intrapreneuring*, New York: Harper Row.

Prabhaker, Paul R., Joel D. Goldhar, and David Lei (1995), "Marketing Implications of Newer Manufacturing Technologies," *Journal of Business & Industrial Marketing*, 10, 48–58.

Provitera, Michael J. (1995), "Sales Management and Sales Teamwork," *American Marketing Association Summer Proceedings*, 176–84.

Ray, Darrel and Howard Bronstein (1995), *Teaming Up: Making the Transition to a Self-directed, Team-based Organization*, New York: McGraw Hill.

Raymond, Louis (1990), "Organizational Context and Information System Success: A Contingency Approach," *Journal of Management Information Systems*, 6 (Spring), 3–20.

Reiste, Kristin K. and Al Hubrich (1995), "Frigidaire Experience," *National Productivity Review*, 14 (Autumn), 45–55.

Schellhardt, Timothy D. (1999), "Some Technology Temps Fare Even Better Than Full-timers," *The Wall Street Journal*, 103 (January 5), B1-B8.

Schlender, Brent (1998), "The Three Faces of Steve," *Fortune*, 138 (November 9), 96–104.

Senn, James A. (1992), "The Myths of Strategic Systems," *Information Systems Management*, 9 (Summer), 7–12.

Shapiro, B. F. (1988), "What the Hell is Market-oriented?" *Harvard Business Review*, 66 (November-December), 119–25.

Shapiro, B. F. (1987), *The New Intimacy*, Boston, MA: Harvard Business School Publishing Division.

Simmel, G. (1950), *The Sociology of Georg Simmel*, (trans. by K. H. Wolff), Glencoe, IL: Free Press.

Simpson, Roy L. (1997), "Technology and the Potential for Entrepreneurship," *Nursing Management*, 28 (October), 24–25.

Sinclair, S. A. and D. H. Cohen (1992), "Adoption of Continuous Processing Technologies: Its Strategic Importance in Standardized Industrial Product Markets," *Journal of Business Research*, 24 (May), 209–24.

Solomon, Charlene Marmer (1995), "Global Teams: The Ultimate Collaboration," *Personnel Journal*, 74 (September), 49–58.

Stearns, Timothy M. and Gearld E. Hills (1996), "Entrepreneurship and New Firm Development: A Definitional Introduction," *Journal of Business Research*, 36 (May), 1–4.

Steinberg, Margery and Richard E. Plank (1987), "Expert Systems: The Integrative Sales Management Tool of the Future," *Journal of the Academy of Marketing Science*, 15 (Summer), 55–62.

Stern, Gary M. (1996), "Young Entrepreneurs Make Their Mark," *Nation's Business*, 84 (August), 49–51.

Stokes, Stewart L., Jr. (1995), Rewards and Recognition for Teams," *Information Systems Management*, 12 (Summer), 61–65.

Stone, Robert W. and David J. Good (1995), "Expert Systems in the Marketing Organization," *Industrial Management & Data Systems*, 95(4), 3–7.

Taylor, Chris (1998), "Cybershop," *Time* (November 23), 142.

Thorn, R. G., J. C. Guynes, and C. S. Guynes (1990), "Strategic Operational Issues for the Successful Information Center," *Journal of Information Systems Management*, 7 (Spring), 15–22.

Tjosvold, Dean and Mary M. Tjosvold (1993), *The Emerging Leader: Ways to a Stronger Team*, New York: Lexington Books.

Tubbs, Stewart L. (1988), *A Systems Approach to Small Group Interaction*, New York: Random House.

Tuck, Larry (1998), "Preaching to the Choir" *Sales and Field Force Automation*, 2 (December), 8.

Turnipseed, D. L., O. M. Burns, and F. J. Hodges (1991), "Attitudes Towards Computers in an Information-intensive Environment: A Field Study of the Insurance Industry," *Journal of Applied Business Research*, 7 (Fall), 123–30.

Tyrer, Kathy (1994), "Marc Pujalet," *Adweek*, 35 (November 14), 40.

Van de Ven, A. and M. S. Poole (1995), "Explaining Development and Change in Organizations," *Academy of Management Review*, 20 (July), 510–40.

Van Gaasbeck, Richard (1993), "Marketers Can't Afford To Invest in Personal Sales Calls." *Marketing News*, 27 (September 13), 22.

Varney, Glenn H. (1989), *Building Productive Teams*, San Francisco, CA: Jossey-Bass.

Webster, Frederick E., Jr. (1994), "Defining the New Marketing Concept," *Marketing Management*, 2, 22–31.

Webster, Frederick E., Jr. (1992), "The Changing Role of Marketing in the Corporation." *Journal of Marketing*, 56 (October), 1–17.

Wiewel, W. and A Hunter (1985), "The Interorganizational Network as a Resource," *Administrative Science Quarterly*, 30, 482–96.

Yoon, Youngohc, Tor Guimaraes, and Quinton O'Neal (1995), "Exploring the Factors Associated with Expert Systems Success," *MIS Quarterly*, 19 (March), 83–106.

Zenger, John H., Ed Musselwhite, Kathleen Hurson, and Craig Perrin (1994), *Leading Teams: Mastering the New Role*, Homewood, IL: Business One Irwin.

Author Index

Subject Index

ABOUT THE AUTHORS

David J. Good has extensive experience in the strategic and operational use of technology. Previously with Sprint, AT&T, and Business Systems Management, Dr. Good focused on the utilization of technology to gain a competitive advantage. He is currently Professor of Marketing at Grand Valley State University in Grand Rapids, Michigan.

Roberta J. Schultz is on the graduate faculty in Marketing for Western Michigan University at Grand Rapids. Previously with Southwestern Bell and American Bell in marketing to large business-to-business markets, Dr. Schultz worked closely with a variety of large technology users.

ISBN 1-56720-244-6

EAN

9 781567 202441

90000>

HARDCOVER BAR CODE